Commercial
Fragrance Bottles

PARFUM
POUR
BRUNES

LIONCEAU
PARIS

Commercial
Fragrance Bottles

Joanne Dubbs Ball ✳ Dorothy Hehl Torem

77 Lower Valley Road, Atglen, PA 19310

Dedication

On behalf of parfum and flacon collectors everywhere, we dedicate this book to those special individuals, past and present, who have tempted us not only with these magical scents but also with the charm and beauty of the bottles that housed them. Only through the imagination and genius of all of them was this effort possible.

Acknowledgments

Special thanks to Ken Leach and Richard Peters of *Gallery 47*, New York City, for their guidance and assistance, as well as to Marjorie Ambrogia of Coty Inc., Kim Friedman and Chris Mohnan of Guerlain Inc., and Debra LaGattuta of Parfums Givenchy; our gratitude also to Patricia Coutts Bagnall, Annie Bower, Robin Cerio, Marion Cohen, Joy Esterson, Alyson Torem French, Elizabeth Hehl Gary, Renee Gold, Mary Gorman, Mike Gross, Jackie and Barbara Hehl, Helene Holland, Marge Levy, Minka Ludeke, Donna Lucente, Magi Matola, Juliet Weber Reid, Bob Simas of *East Greenwich Photo*, Conrad Vout, Jan Walker of *Lord & Taylor*, and Nancy Wedderspoon.

Our gratitude to Regine de Robien of *Beaute Divine* in Paris for sharing her interview and special treasures with us; also to Catherine Adamov, Tatiana Abbey, and Charles and Suzy Torem.

Copyright © 1993 by Joanne Dubbs Ball and Dorothy Hehl Torem
Library of Congress Catalog Number: 93-85222
Photographs by Dorothy Hehl Torem

Printed in the United States of America.
ISBN: 0-88740-556-8
We are interested in hearing from authors with book ideas on related topics.

Published by Schiffer Publishing Ltd.
77 Lower Valley Road
Atglen, PA 19310
Please write for a free catalog.
This book may be purchased from the publisher.
Please include $2.95 postage.
Try your bookstore first.

Contents

Foreword

The waning decades of the 20th century have generated renewed interest in collectibles from the past, including much enthusiasm for commercial perfume bottles, a time-honored staple of boudoirs and dressing tables for centuries. Not surprisingly, many of these bottles are now more costly than their contents once were. The value of packaging as a marketing technique was recognized by successful merchandisers early on, and what encases the product has frequently proven to be just as important to consumers and collectors as the fluid inside.

Included in this book will be the beauty of the most opulent presentations of yesteryear, many of which are the aficionado's "Mount Everest," the *creme de la creme* of perfume bottles. They are among the most "important" commercial fragrance bottles–rare, ornate, and costly. Many of them were made by the finest artisans of this or any time.

While these exquisite pieces are apt to be the bottles most fervently sought, the thrill of uncovering whimsical items that once sold for less than a dollar or two cannot be overlooked. A host of sophisticated collectors consider these off-beat entrants just as desirable as their more "elegant" counterparts. For that reason, and because the public's ever-growing fascination with perfume bottles covers the entire spectrum of commercial production, this book will present a broad range of perfumes and colognes. As avid collectors of *anything* will vouch, just about *everything* is important to someone! Scattered throughout "collectors' land" is an eclectic mix of those who covet the rare and costly, as well as others who find delight in the charm of an amusing container reminiscent of Saturday outings to the local five and ten cent store.

Whatever the fragrance–whether in a fancy case in a Fifth Avenue department store or in a cardboard box on the counter of a cluttered five and dime–each offers an insight into the tenor of the times that nurtured it. Every generation has spawned its "haves" and "have nots"–and, above all, the vast middle ground that bridged the two. But no matter where they lived, with whom they associated, or what they could afford, most women took pleasure in the real or imagined luxury of their favorite scents.

Astute manufacturers were attuned to the widely differing economic and cultural markets, and chose their niches accordingly. On one hand, there were fancy French and "foreign-inspired" fragrances whose names alone invited the public to sample...and purchase. On the other, the names of some manufacturers' offerings straightforwardly "told it like it was." Philadelphia's Alfred B. Taylor reached the ordinary women who comprised most of the 1870s' female population with the bluntly-named *Twenty-Five Scent Cologne.* In the Depression days of the 1930s, the Special Purpose Perfume Company of Chicago minced no words either, skipping all flowery sentiments as they marketed fragrances geared to particular occasions, like simply *Birthday Perfume*!

Simplistics aside, collectors continue to search without respite for items that remind them of the past. A lovely scent and the curve of a beautiful bottle–like treasured photographs or a romantic tune of yesteryear–are imbued with a magical, even sensual, quality, capable of transporting the present into the past. Empty or full, the bottle carries indelible impressions invisible to the naked eye.

Who hasn't unexpectedly smelled a long-forgotten fragrance or uncovered a special bottle from days gone by and been flooded with memories? *"Oh, that's what I wore at my engagement party," "How grown-up I felt when I dabbed a drop behind each ear before my first prom,"* or *"I remember that beautiful bottle on my mother's dressing table when I was a child...she always smelled so nice when she tucked me in at night."* Fragrance is indeed far more than an olfactory sensation it is the elixir of dreams! How fortunate we are that although the precious, sweet-smelling fluid may be just a memory, its container is able to evoke such diverse and personal feelings.

During the past century, there have been hundreds of manufacturers and thousands upon thousands of trademarked scents, each garnering its own niche in the fragrance market, no matter how short-lived. But, as today's consumer preferences prove, there's always room for one more, as women the world over anxiously await the latest entrant.

Perfume flacons spanning the century. The center cut-glass, metal-topped container is from the turn of the century; the round bottle-shaped container has center faux amythyst stones and is an attractive Victorian-style brooch, probably from the 1920s or Thirties. The purse-size parfum container on right is engraved sterling with a hinged top that releases the bottle. A matron of honor gift in 1949, it originally came with a miniature sterling silver funnel.

Cut glass Victorian scent vial with
metal, spring top.

As with more prosaic companies and products, the "ebb and flow" of the audience's enthusiasm caused many perfumeries and their individual offerings to come and go. Countless perfumes that once triumphantly rode the crest of success no longer exist...but, thankfully for the collector, the bottle and packaging remain as precious remnants of times past. Other fragrances have long since been established as classics, popular decade after decade. In some instances the bottle design has remained the same, but in others the container is no longer like its predecessors, and over the years many different presentations have housed the same fragrance.

In this book, a small sampling of relatively new fragrance entries is also shown. Although space and other restraints do not permit displaying all of the particularly unique and beautiful examples that presently grace the counters and shelves of boutiques and department stores, this will serve as a representative collection of lovely and artistic current bottles. Many will undoubtedly become collectibles of the future, and are surely worthy of our admiration today.

Whether newly added to a perfumery's repertoire or a treasured member of their archives, each flacon serves as a testimonial to the ingenuity of its designer and manufacturer. Collectively, these artisans have been responsible for delighting the public with an awesome array of unique bottles to house the scents that play such an important, yet subtle, role in the aura of those who wear them. The innate desire of women to experiment, to enjoy, and, above all, to enhance the feminine mystique, is timeless. Clothing and accessories have the power to create personalized fashion statements; so too do the fragrances with which we surround ourselves, for they also serve as building blocks in the creation of each woman's individual persona.

Presentation is everything...or at least *just about everything*...as what follows will clearly attest.

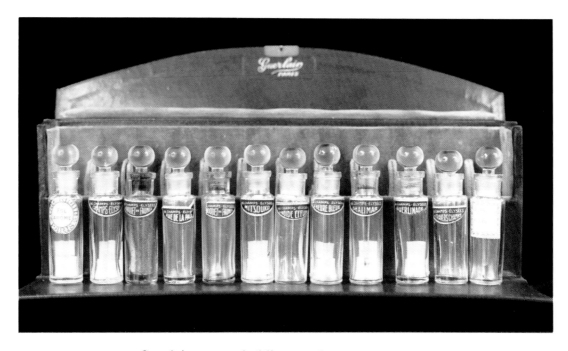

Guerlain tester holding twelve
fragrances; late 1920s; 2-3/4".

Section One-
The Art of Fragrance
All Bottled Up

A woman who doesn't wear perfume has no future. Paul Valery

Prominent names in the history of the fragrance industry could not possibly be covered in detail in one volume. Some makers, however, are significant because of the particular longevity they have enjoyed in the field. Others are remarkable for their unflagging dedication to providing a wide spectrum of interesting scents, and to assuaging women's constant desire for something new and different. The members of this select group will be used as examples on behalf of the myriad of others which–each in its own special way–brought unique skills to the illustrious "art of fragrance."

Every endeavor has its pioneers. Those in the annals of the parfum industry are no exception. At the forefront of these trail-blazing giants are the many parfumeries that devoted their efforts exclusively to creating the magical potions that caused many an unsuspecting male to fall under a woman's spell. But, in addition to these, there were pioneers in many diverse categories of enterprise. Proprietors of apothecaries became involved, and later, pharmaceutical companies. Renowned couturiers came to recognize the subtle yet important blending of fashion and fragrance and began production of their own scents. Emporiums perceived the marketing potential in attaching their highly-respected names to scents that would, they hoped, be faithfully purchased by their steady stream of loyal customers. When cosmetic, soap and lotion companies became aware of untapped commercial opportunities in the perfume field, they crossed the fine line between what a woman smoothed over her face and what she splashed or dabbed on her body!

Parfums...First and Foremost

Prominent among this group of early purists–and still a major contributor to modern-day parfums–is the House of Guerlain, the oldest family-owned fragrance company in the world. Established in 1828 by chemist-doctor Pierre Francoise Guerlain, the company's initial success was as a "perfumer and Purveyor of smelling salts," a necessity for any genteel lady's dressing table. In their factory on the outskirts of Paris, Guerlain developed not only bottled scents but also a vast array of complementary lotions and powders, all certain to please their French clientele.

In 1861 Guerlain's eldest son Aime joined the firm, followed three years later by his brother Gabriel. Before the turn of the century, they had produced a plethora of scents that were enormously popular with Continental women. All had delightful names characteristic of the times: *Cuir de Russie, Dix Petals de Roses, Fleur de Itale, Jardins de Bagatelle* and *Rococo a la Parisienne*. As a logical outgrowth of their expertise in fragrance, Guerlain expanded its product base in the early 20th century to include cosmetics and skin care products. These lines have proved equally popular, and the company continues to promote innovative additions year after year, always anticipating and meeting the trends of an ever-changing market.

Following their father's death in 1933, Gabriel's sons Pierre and Jacque entered the business, and their sons, Raymond, Jean-Pierre, Jean Jacques and Marcel succeeded them. This family devotion to the business and the control such care has produced gives the House of Guerlain a depth of expertise and family pride –traits that are evident to this day. The results are impressive and startling in their consistency...fragrance after fragrance, each a masterpiece of the perfumer's art.

Since its inception, the House of Guerlain has been prescient in divining the important yet often elusive connection between the mystique of a beautiful scent and the trends of fashion, music, art and even politics. They have consistently succeeded in translating their insights into perfumes that captured the mood and aura of the times.

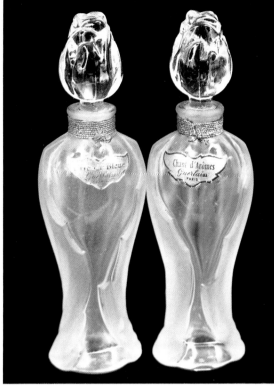

L'Heure Bleue and *Chant d'Aromes;* Guerlain; frosted Lalique-style bottles with flower bud tops; same bottle design used for *L'Heure Bleue* (introduced in 1912), *Mitsouko* (introduced in 1919), and Chant d'Aromes (1962).

The Guerlain family tree.

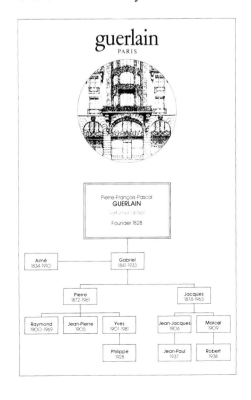

L'Heure Bleu; 4" Baccarat bottle in intricately designed presentation case with an "Old World flavor"; Guerlain; introduced in 1912.

Cologne de Coq; one of Guerlain's early fragrances, introduced in 1894; 6-1/4" bottle. This design also housed 1853's Eau De Cologne Imperiale, which was created for the Empress Eugenie and was covered with etchings of bees, the symbol of the Napoleonic Empire.

Several fragrances are particularly strong examples of this ability. The earliest is *Jicky*, introduced in 1889 as a loving tribute to Aime's favorite nephew, Jacques, and the nickname Aime had playfully bestowed on him. Today, *Jicky* has the unique distinction of being the oldest Guerlain fragrance still on the market. This floral scent was based on new scientific discoveries in distillation, and it remains an icon–the first *modern* perfume.

In 1912, Guerlain introduced *L'Heure Bleue*, a nostalgic, now classic fragrance of romantic innocence steeped in the gentle hues of twilight. A decade later, responding to a world-sweeping infatuation with all things Oriental, *Mitsouko* made its debut. But perhaps the most outstanding example is *Shalimar*, quite possibly Guerlain's most famous fragrance. It created a sensation in 1925, and its popularity continues into the last decade of the 20th century, giving credence to the timelessness of a great fragrance.

Like *Mitsouko, Shalimar* was conceived in response to the Persian, Middle- and Far-Eastern influences that dominated so many areas of the prevailing 1920s lifestyle. In fashion, fabrics, interior design and even the movies–a la the mystique of *The Sheik*, Rudolph Valentino–the magnetism of this exotic, opulent fantasy world made its way into the hearts and minds of the women of the world. *Shalimar* was there to add its own glamour to the scene!

Guerlain was also influenced by the literature of the day. One example of their *au courant* attitude can be found in their classic 1933 fragrance *Vol de Nuit*. This perfume was inspired by French novelist Antoine de Saint-Exupery's award-winning novel of the same name, published in French in 1931 and translated into English as *Night Flight* in 1932.

Representing the fourth generation of Guerlains, Jean Paul Guerlain (a great-great-grandson of Pierre Guerlain) now heads the House, involving yet another generation, and bringing the total to an amazing five! Today Jean Paul is the company's master perfumer, having created such fragrances as *Vetiver, Habit Rouge, Chamade* and *Samsara*.

With over 200 perfumes currently to their credit, the House of Guerlain is unflagging in its determination to maintain the high standards that formed the foundation upon which Pierre Guerlain's built his fledgling company so many years ago...the standards that continue to epitomize quality, style and elegance. It only follows that fragrance lovers the world over can look forward to 200 more!

Another of the earliest in this group of parfum entrepreneurs was D'Orsay, a French company established in the 1830s. Their offerings did not reach the U.S. market until early in the 20th century, but by then American women were already drawn to the images of magnetic (and even naughty) sexuality that were prompted by the mere mention of French women–and the men who pursued them! Fascinated women, lured by the idea of the "French experience," surrounded themselves in tittilating clouds of fragrance with a "decidedly French, decidedly Continental" flair. The perfumes of choice included *Ambre d'Orsay, Bouquet d'Orsay* and *Chevalier d'Orsay*.

D'Orsay was closely followed by Molinard, a French fragrance house established in 1849. Molinard offered enchanting scents in exquisite bottles, many the works of Rene Lalique, Baccarat and other artists.

Founded in 1903 by Ernest Daltroff, the House of Caron was also a prominent name on the early French perfume scene. However, Caron's marketing took an unusual turn, for their products were exported to England, South America, and the United States for nearly thirty years before becoming readily available to their own countrymen. One of Caron's earliest entrants, *Narcisse Noir*, was an instant success in 1912, and the bottle, with its unique floral stopper, has become a much-copied classic. Established in 1885, Lentheric was yet another French enterprise that became a smashing success in the United States after the introduction of their fragrances in the 1920s. Offerings by the venerable houses of Corday and Lancome received similarly enthusiastic receptions.

Although French perfume had become almost synonymous with fragrance, many U.S. companies also competed for "fragrance dollars." Most, however, were not players to be reckoned with until well into the 20th century. One notable exception was Solon Palmer, who founded the Cincinnati perfumerie bearing his name in the mid-19th century.

Palmer offered a plethora of scents, including *India Bouquet* in 1878, *Lilac Sweets* in 1890, and *Baby Ruth* in 1892, all of which captured the fancy of American women. Palmer was attuned to the floral themes so popular early in the century, and in 1905 introduced *Garland of Roses* and *Garland of Violets*. Responding to cultural moods and infatuations, the company remained current with offerings like *Egyptian Lotus, Ihlang Ihlang* and *Marvel of Peru* in the Twenties, fashion- and glamour-oriented *Dress Parade* in the Thirties, and the innocence of *Centennial Bouquet* in the Forties.

Renowned for its contributions to American perfumes, the Solon Palmer company has yet another distinction, for it was the first fragrance company to recognize the value of using traveling salesmen to tout their wares!

Other U.S. companies joined the competition for market share in the 20th century. These included the "dynasty" of Prince Matchabelli, founded in New York City in the 1920s. The company cleverly used the Matchabelli "royal crown" as its trademark, and fragrance after fragrance debuted in similarly-designed bottles–a brilliant move. A decade later, the New York Blanchard and Charbert companies entered the market. At the same time, three thousand miles to the west, the firm of De Hariot chose Hollywood as the obvious location for launching glamourous perfume products. The Forties saw the rise of other contenders in disparate locations, including Angelique, a Connecticut-based company, and Anjou, based in Illinois.

By any standards, Coty has earned its "front and center" position among enterprises that have built their reputations in the field of fragrance *and* cosmetics. However, as was the case with many of their illustrious counterparts like Guerlain, Lentheric and Lancome, fragrances came *first* and not as an adjunct to cosmetics or couture.

Coty's founder, Francoise Coty, bears a large share of the credit for bringing the "modern-day" art of perfumery–and much of what that entails–into the 20th century. Not only did he expand its market, but he imbued fragrance with a magical splendor it had rarely been afforded since the time of ancient civilizations.

First and foremost, Monsieur Coty was endowed with what is known as "a nose," and this gift directed his interest, however subliminally, to the chemical elements of fragrances. However, Coty might never have discovered this latent talent were it not for his friendship with a chemist-shopkeeper, whose inept attempts to sell his own scents were a dismal failure. The gentleman had carefully concocted the fragrances, but merchandised them in unattractive, inexpensive bottles. Monsieur Coty's instant realization that the two elements–fragrance *and* packaging–were interdependent led to his own tentative explorations into the business of making and marketing perfumes. The results were to have an enormous impact on the entire industry.

Coty proceeded on the assumption that fragrances should be elevated to luxury status, for, although his entrepreneurship was built on his "nose," it was also founded on the premise that luxuries demand skillful presentation if they are to succeed. This meant not only bottles of exquisite design but boxes, labels, even papers that conveyed an image of exclusivity. The bottles he chose were works of art, and those created by artisans like Baccarat and jewelry designer René Lalique became "jewels" in their own right.

Coty's business acumen opened doors and gained him the assistance of several essential oil houses, including Givaudan and Company, which remains to this day an important supplier of oils worldwide. Without their financial assistance to move his venture forward–and, above all, without that "nose"–much of what happened after could never have occurred. Luckily, however, Coty's ability to recognize and understand the finite nuances of smell brought each element to fruition–products that appealed to the eyes as well as to the olfactory senses. Thus, Coty attended not only to the fragrance itself, but also to its presentation in the form of an object that could be touched, held, and appreciated by the eyes.

In addition to smell, sight, and feel, there was another dimension that Monsieur Coty considered equally important to the success of his product–its name. And, thus, he added another sense, the auditory, to the overall packaging concept. Once again, his innovative thinking played a major role in what was to follow, for by introducing "fantasy" names–with their romantic, melodious, and sometimes mysterious sounds, all of which were pleasing and seductive to the ear–each new entrant added another stone to the foundation upon which The House of Coty was built.

The tale of the entrance of the House of Coty into Parisienne emporiums is a delightful one. We are told that when Monsieur Coty approached the Louvre department store with a new creation called *La Rose Jacqueminot*, he was summarily dismissed. As he made his disheartened exit, the bottle dropped from his hands and crashed to the floor–perhaps accidentally, though one would like to think the slip was deliberate–and its fragrant contents engulfed the patrons, who immediately demanded to know where it could be purchased.

Paris de Coty; introduced in 1921.

L'Origan; Coty; 1909.

Ambre Antique; Coty; 1913.

L'Origan de Coty; shagreen box, 2-1/4" Lalique bottle. Introduced in 1909, this is a later presentation.

The rest is history. That one broken bottle was responsible for launching the Coty name into the hearts of women worldwide–and into the prominence it so richly deserves in any telling of the fragrance story. What woman of this or the past several generations has not at one time or another been intrigued by an exotically-named Coty scent, like *Ambre Antique, Emeraude* or *L'Origan*? Over the years, she most likely either purchased or expectantly opened a gift of one, for since 1904 the House of Coty has introduced nearly one hundred fragrances, all designed to captivate these ladies–and their gentlemen! Many of their scents are classics that remain as popular today as when first introduced–a continuing tribute to Coty and his distinguished peers, each of whom "made his mark" with fragrances that succeeded in crossing all generational barriers. Also, virtually non-existent is the woman who doesn't recognize the classically beautiful Coty Airspun powder box, for it was, or still remains, a staple of her dressing table...or her mother's or grandmother's. Indeed, that incomparable Airspun box–designed by Leonard Bakst, who was also responsible for the stage settings and costumes of the first Ballet Russe–has more than withstood the test of time. It is a venerated classic, not only in its category but throughout the entire spectrum of cosmetics.

Couture and Fragrances

In addition to geniuses like Pierre Guerlain and Francois Coty, who were primarily perfumers and expanded their businesses from that base, there were talented individuals who gained prominence in other professions, and only later recognized the value of adding fragrances to their repertoire. However, they too achieved success not simply by introducing these scents but by recognizing the power of innovative presentation and packaging in any competitive venture.

Chief among these was the master couturier Paul Poiret (not to be confused with the French perfumery also named Poiret). Born in France in 1879, Poiret succeeded in expanding couture to yet another dimension, for he was also an artist, a designer of theatrical costuming, and a gentleman of superior vision. Not only did Poiret's enlighted genius "scoop" many of his contemporaries in the fashion world, but he was also several steps ahead when it came to fragrance. For "...at a single stroke he would extend the field of fashion to include perfume, cosmetics and interior design and...he was the only Paris couturier to market perfume for another ten years."[1] In a daring move, considering the staid environment of 1911, Poiret introduced his own fragrances, using the tradenames "Rosine and Martine." Individual scents were labeled with names like *Maharahjah, Alladin, Borgia* and *Fanfan la Tulipe*.

The bottles for these delightful scents, along with their marketing presentations, have been described as "supreme works of art," often very elaborately presented. For example,

> In one instance, each flacon was wrapped in a beautifully colored handkerchief designed to match the mood of the buyer, blending the color with the fragrance. And, as the *piece de resistance*, a wide ring designed to slip over one's glove secured the handkerchief to the container it covered. Other bottles were of metal with bold designs in *bas relief* and topped with huge ivory stoppers. The exquisite patterns of Poiret's powder boxes were visually astounding, their heavy tassels covering large dome-shaped lids, like treasure chests begging to be opened.[2]

Poiret's marketing skills were also ahead of their time:

> To promote his perfumes at one couturier showing–in what was probably a warm and airless pre-air-conditioning salon–each female attendee was presented with a fan that wafted one of Poiret's scents from a disc identifying it by name as she fluttered it in front of her flushed face!"[3]

The interaction between fashion and fragrance has been a continuing one. Although fashion and accessories are the outward evidence of couturiers' talents, Poiret and many of his peers were quick to recognize the invisible link between fragrance and the female psyche, a link that presented enormous marketing opportunities. Suffice it to say that although his products have not been marketed for many decades, the legacy Poiret left behind–in fashion as well as in fragrance–is enormous.

Poiret was not the only couturier to "smell the roses" and offer them to Madame with verve and imagination. Another was Charles Worth, who, although British, is recognized as the founder of French couture. He tossed his hat into the fragrance ring with the introduction of such scents as *Sans Adieu, Vers Le Jour, Je Reviens,* and *Honeysuckle* in the Twenties and Thirties. The Worth name offered a veritable parade of new fragrances throughout the intervening decades, culminating in the Seventies with *Fleurs Fraiches* and *Miss Worth.*

Gabrielle "Coco" Chanel established a niche that has become the most enduring among that early group of couturier "pioneers." Today, *Chanel No. 5* remains a permanent and on-going legend in the fairy tale history of Chanel...and in the fragrance industry. Chanel was very superstitious about numbers. Thus, *Chanel No. 5* was conceived when Chanel happened to choose the fifth perfume sample offered her by its designer, Ernest Beaux, one of the greatest names in perfume at that time. The bottle was marked simply "5," and that was enough for Chanel!

The scent that became *Chanel No. 5*–now an almost archtypical name for perfume itself–contained aldehyde and synthetic substances along with natural essences. Its success put the prejudice that existed against aldehyde finally and forever to rest. Introduced in Europe in 1921 and in the United States three years later, the classic *Chanel No. 5* bottle, manufactured by Brosse, has been ensconced in New York's Museum of Modern Art since 1959.

The name *Chanel No. 5* was such a quintessential French perfume that following the liberation of Paris in World War II, a line of American GIs over 300 yards long snaked down the avenue from Chanel's headquarters at 31 rue Cambon. There they waited patiently to purchase a treasured gift of *Chanel No. 5* for girlfriends, wives, and mothers back home.

Some fifty years after *Chanel No. 5*'s introduction, and a year before Madame Chanel's death in 1972, *No. 19* was introduced. Whether "5" or "19," numbers still held a particular magic for Chanel (all of whose couture showings occurred on the fifth of the month). In light of the results, who could dispute her superstition!

Fashion maven Elsa Schiaparelli was fast on Chanel's heels, presenting fragrance after fragrance from the early Thirties into the Fifties, with charming names like *Salud, Shocking, Sleeping* and *Souci* in the Thirties, *Sans Souci, Radiance, Snuff, Spanking, Stratosphere* and *Zut* among others in the Forties, and *Si, Succes Fou, Voyageur* and *Spring* and *Summer* in the Fifties.

Hattie Carnegie carried the mystique of "the little black dress" into the inner sanctum of fragrance with the simply-named *Hattie Carnegie* in the late Twenties, and *Miss Hattie,* as well as others, in the Fifties and Sixties. During these latter decades the Carnegie perfume division was headed by her nephew, the late Irving Apisdorf, whose marketing skills in both the fragrance and jewelry lines brought an exciting new dimension to Carnegie's accomplishments. These scents frequently incorporated colors into their names, like *Carnegie Blue, Carnegie Pink, Carte Bleue* and *Carte Verte.*

Nettie Rosenstein, renowned for her beautiful fashions and elegant jewelry, tempted the Forties' and Fifties' woman with fragrances like *Tianne, Fleurs D'Elle,* and *Odalisque.* Adele Simpson brought them the aptly-named *Introduction,* followed by *Collage.*

The list of other couture giants who proffered their own exclusive entrants in this "potpourri of fragrance" reads like a veritable "who's who" of fashion. In addition to the illlustrious Madame Vionnet, such luminaries as Balmain, Lanvin, Maurice Blanchet, Lucien Lelong, Molyneux, Jacques Fath, Dior, Givenchy, Adrian, Cardin, Courreges, Patou, Nina Ricci, Rochas, Saint Laurent, Oscar de la Renta, Valentino, Karl Lagerfeld, Ralph Lauren and a host of others have methodically presented a seemingly endless array of fragrances to tempt and delight! In the Eighties and Nineties, such fashion luminaries as Calvin Klein, Romeo Gigli, Donna Karan and Bob Mackie joined the couture-fragrance bandwagon, with others undoubtedly waiting expectantly in the wings!

Hubert de Givenchy provides an outstanding example of the modern day, couture-fragrance connection. As a young man he spent seven years apprenticing with such renowned couturiers as Jacques Fath, Lucien Lelong and Elsa Schiaparelli, and in 1951, at age 24, he established his own couture house. Blessed with a particular brilliance in adapting materials to the spirit of the times, he has earned his reputation as "the man who can't make a mistake." Responsible for creating couture offerings for many of the world's best dressed women, including the Duchess of Windsor, Grace Kelly, Jacqueline Onassis, and Audrey Hepburn, it logically followed that in 1957 the gamin-like Hepburn would inspire his first fragrance, *L'Interdit.*

Snuff; 5" pipe with pouch; Schiaparelli's fragrance for men, introduced in 1940.

Considering perfume to be the crowning touch of total elegance, Givenchy has introduced new fragrances one after another in the years since. In a bold step that few if any had ever taken before, Givenchy captured yet another unexpected market in the late Eighties when he launched a luxurious scent called *Ptisbenbon* for a new genre of users–infants and toddlers!

Cosmetics and Fragrances

Whether in their neighborhood drug store, a department store in middle America, or an exclusive boutique on Fifth Avenue, women from all walks of life were afforded the opportunity to sample a myriad of fragrance choices while shopping for their favorite cosmetics. Like the instinctive melding with couture, the cosmetic-fragrance connection was a "match made in heaven," and its success has sent an indisputable message: fashion, cosmetics, and fragrance are inextricably bound together! Thus, it was only logical that retailers who merchandised all or some of these under one roof would happily avail themselves of this ready-made market.

One of the industry's major innovators, Bourjois, also had its beginnings in the late 1800s, and is responsible for singlehandedly initiating two major cosmetic breakthroughs that are now taken for granted. Like everything else, though, someone had to do it first...and in the case of dry rouge (conceived in 1890) and the powder compact, Bourjois must take a bow!

From that auspicious beginning, the list of Bourjois fragrances expanded in short order–*Ashes of Violets* and *Ashes of Sandal* in 1913, followed by a series of others that endured through the 1950s. But who has not seen, touched, smelled, or at least heard of *Evening in Paris*, indisputably the most famous of all? Among the most popular fragrances of the 20th century, it has probably been enjoyed by the greatest number of women, many of modest means. Moreover, it has been presented in an enormous array of innovative packages–from sumptious presentation boxes replete with perfumes and talcs to simple and relatively inexpensive offerings. They were all designed to make the perfect gift from husband to wife, suitor to girlfriend, or daughter to mother. Following its introduction in 1929, *Evening in Paris* became an almost generic scent, redolent of romantic flights of fancy. The name struck a receptive chord in the minds and hearts of women during the stark times of the Great Depression and World War II. Even today, the sight or mention of *Evening in Paris* conjures up–in both sexes–poignant associations from days long past of that famous blue bottle or powder box, with the majestic Eiffel Tower dramatically displayed against a starlit sky.

Richard Hudnut was another of the shining stars of the "cosmetic-fragrance connection," establishing his products' popularity before the turn of the century and maintaining the momentum decade after decade thereafter...from scents like *Hudnutine* in 1893, *Extreme Violet* in 1895, *Aimee* and *Cardinal* in 1902 to more modern entrants like *Yanky Clover, Firebrand* and *Frozen Champagne* in the Forties, and *Young Folks, Monkey Business* and *Charmed Circle* in the "fabulous" Fifties.

Others, large and small–including illustrious names like Charles of the Ritz, Helena Rubenstein (The House of Gourielli), Elizabeth Arden, Frances Denny, Jacqueline Cochran, DuBarry, Revlon, Estee Lauder, Germaine Monteil, Alexandra de Markoff, and Max Factor–were also "factors" to be reckoned with in the fragrance sweepstakes.

Retailers and Fragrances

The "sweet smell of success" was reason enough for countless retailers–who were, of course, able to expend the dollars and manpower necessary–to jump aboard the fragrance merry-go-round. Surprisingly, several retailing giants had recognized this untapped potential well before the turn the century. John Wanamaker of Philadelphia appears to be the first, introducing *Queen Mary* in 1881 and *Cartwright* in 1883. These were followed by *Claire, Ye Ye, Fleur D'Ord* and *Reine Marie* in 1910, *Charme d'Amour* in 1917, plus an array of others, continuing into the 1920s.

Close on Wanamaker's heels was the May Department Store group with the presentation of its flagship brand, *Anita*, in 1888. Over several decades, Henri Bendel gave its customers an impressive list of fragrances: *Un Peu d'elle* in 1915; *No. 7,*

Gout du Jour, Chute D'un Ange, Cinque Triple Cinque, Jasmin de Japan, and *Ma Rose, Ma Violette,* and *Mon Jasmin* in the Twenties; *Dites Moi Oui, Etoile, Filante, Sans-gene, Si Rare, Zita, Suede,* and *10 West* (named for their location on 57th Street in New York) in the Thirties; and *Checkmate* and *White Freezia* in the Forties.

New York's B. Altman had *Premier Amour, Sans Egal* and *Tout Seu* in the Twenties. Lord and Taylor introduced *J'en Rene* and *L'Esprit du Printempts* in 1927, and Abraham & Straus entered the arena with *Mirabelle* in 1936. In sunny California some ten years later, Bullocks gave its customers *L'Ete du Jardin* and *Palm Springs,* while on the opposite coast, Bergdorf Goodman tempted their clientele with *No. 101* in 1927, *Flower Shower* in 1948, and *Fireworks* and *Nandi* in the Fifties.

The list of "players" in this category was nationwide in scope, since it provided a highly successful marketing technique for enterprising retailers who recognized the potential and swiftly acted upon it...scent after scent after scent!

Pharmaceuticals, Soaps, Lotions ...and Fragrances

It was inevitable that pharmaceutical houses, with laboratories and chemists already in place, would also become attuned to the value of marketing fragrances as an adjunct to over-the-counter drug preparations. Surprisingly, one of the earliest– if not *the* earliest–was an American company, Caswell-Massey of Providence, Rhode Island, founded by Dr. William Hunter in 1752. From the beginning, his pharmaceutical and perfume choices shared equal billing.

The Caswell-Massey clientele list reads like the pages from an American history book. Indeed one could hardly boast more illustrious customers than George Washington, Dolly Madison, and the Marquis de Lafayette! Now in its third century of providing fragrances and matching toilette items to a clientele from all walks of life, the Caswell-Massey tradition remains one of America's oldest and most impressive success stories.

Following a close second in the "earliest" category is the British company Yardley of London, founded in 1770. Also makers of soaps for renowned clients (including the royal family), their flagship scent remains the one most apt to be associated with the Yardley name. It was *Lavender,* introduced in England in the early 1780s, and the first of their repertoire to reach the U.S. marketplace.

In middle America, the Wrisley brothers provide another tale of determination...and success. Their business began in the 1860s with soaps, and some twenty years later they established the permanent headquarters of the Wrisley Company in Chicago. The thriving enterprise quickly became known for its fragrances as well, spanning the decades from 1895's *Colonial* to the 1960s *Magnetique.*

Yet another pharmaceutical company to become involved in perfumerie was Andrew Jergens, an enterprise most apt to be associated with creams and lotions. This company entered the fragrance market early on, with *Aloha* in 1883, and *Zenobia* in 1909.

Founded in New York in 1890, Daggett and Ramsdell was also an apothecary operation that took a back seat to none in the celebrity clientele category, with customers like Lillian Russell and society's "500" passing through their doors. Fragrance after fragrance appeared for six decades thereafter, including *Dagelle* in 1929, *Sonata* in the 1930s, *Arabesque* in 1949, and *French Secret, French Sonata,* and *Miss Teen* in the 1950s.

That grand old American institution, Colgate (later Colgate Palmolive, and Colgate Palmolive-Peet), was a household name in fragrance well before the turn of the century. They introduced *Wedding March* in 1879, followed in rapid succession by many others including *Speciosa* in 1886, *Coleo* and *Fleurette* in 1890, *D'Actylis* in 1901, *Viodora* in 1903, *Week-End* in 1904, *Knickerbocker* in 1905, and a long parade of entrants marching decade after decade into the 1940s.

Even the venerable Lever Brothers began to compete with Colgate for fragrance market share ...as well as for that of laundry soap! The Lever company tempted Victorian ladies as early as the mid-1800s with down-to-earth scents bearing cheerful names like *Sunshine* and *Sunbeam,* and revitalized their fragrance connection a century later with *Dreamy, Happy Time, Private Wire* and *Why Talk.*

On and on they came! Among the larger companies was Beecham's Laboratory, with *Ambrosia* and *Royal English Rose.* United Drug had *Cara Nome* (the name

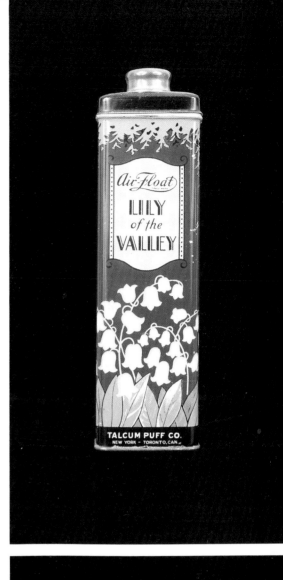

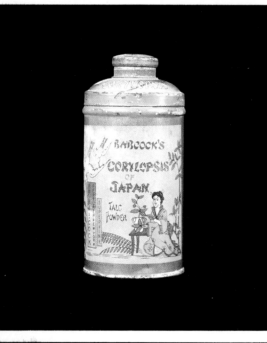

chosen for an entire cosmetic line, and one that remained popular into the Forties, providing many a young lady with an initiation to her first lipstick), as well as individual scents like *Bouquet Dazira*, introduced in 1915, followed by *Truflor*, and *Jonteel* in 1918, and a surfeit of others into the 1920s.

Not to be outdone, the American Druggist Syndicate gave "flappers" of the Roaring Twenties *D'Arline, Delectol* and *Tijade*.

McKesson & Robbins had *Aluria, Florise*, and *Khama* during the same decade, followed by *Canterbury House* in the 1930s, and *Rosemary* and *Lynx* in the Forties. Marketed as a separate entity, *Lucretia Vanderbilt* was their upscale and most popular brand, with an individual fragrance line that included *Gardenia, Jasmin, Sweet Pea, Golden Butterfly* and *Muguet* in the 1930s, and *My Hero* and *Renee* in the Forties. During the same decade, Arrow Laboratories made a tentative entrance into the field with *Mad Hatter*.

Certainly not to be overlooked in this sweeping category is Shulton, which also specialized in soaps and cosmetics. They will long be remembered for two fragrances that must surely be classified among the most widely purchased and highly recognizable scents and packaging of all time–*Old Spice*, introduced in 1936, and *Friendship's Garden* in 1940.

For many of these pharmaceutical houses, the opportunities to introduce other products associated with fragrances served as a viable and lucrative business adjunct–and for still others it became an essential mainstay during this heady time when the public was consumed with its search for just the right "scents for the senses"!

Home Products Companies, the Door-to-Door Salesperson...and Fragrances

At the other end of the spectrum, but certainly not to be overlooked in any recounting of the fragrance story, are companies that touted their products wholly apart from the more commonplace retail environment of the day. Chief among these were Stanley Home Products of Westfield, Massachusetts, and the Fuller Brush Company of Hartford, Connecticut. Both astutely realized that many women, far removed from Fifth Avenue and its environs, would welcome the opportunity to purchase something apt to quicken the senses–a reward of sorts for toiling over a grimy kitchen floor–while considering the qualities of a good mop or broom from their trusted door-to-door salesmen. Understandably, a loyal and lively market for bottled scents was established, thanks to that vast army of *ordinary* housewives, and it proved to be a successful selling technique for decades.

The door-to-door representative was elevated to more specialized status by Avon Products, which made it possible for women to purchase not only cosmetics but a wide assortment of fragrances in the comfort and privacy of their homes. It was a marketing coup that, with variations over the years, shows no sign of diminishing in popularity. Today the interest in old Avon fragrance containers has become a wholly separate collectibles category, with eager buyers searching exclusively for these particularly whimsical examples from the past–and awaiting tomorrow's collectible in the form of new Avon fragrances, for both women and men, that are being introduced yearly.

The Bottle Designers and Manufacturers

No synopsis of the fragrance story would be complete without paying tribute to the bottle designers and manufacturers. They added visual beauty to complement the olfactory sensation of the fragrance, thereby creating a "work of art" that captured the essence of yet another "work of art." In the process, they influenced the success of its contents to a great degree. The sense of smell critiques the scent, but the eye must also be drawn to the bottle, which then becomes a major factor in influencing its purchase.

First are the glass-making and designing geniuses of the French companies that manufactured and in many cases also designed these flacons. Shining like beacons of the glassmakers' art are the illustrious names of Lalique, Baccarat, Lucien Gaillard and J. Viard, as well as Pochet Et Du Courval, and Saint Gobain Desjonqueres. In the United States, glass companies like Wheaton and Carr-Lowry are also responsible for many of the beautiful presentations we so admire today.

The artistic and imaginative creations of the bottle designers continue to infuse the industry with a heritage rich in beauty; each new offering uncovers another level of vitality and luxury. These companies and individuals have played a monumental role in the history of fragrances. In fact, their vision and genius cannot be too highly praised in any accounting of this story. The luminaries of the perfume world have given us so many unforgettable bottles that, unfortunately, crediting all or even most of them is logistically impossible. Several, therefore, will be showcased here to "take a bow" on behalf of the many.

Lalique, for one, is responsible for many of the classic bottles so admired today, including Nina Ricci's *L'Air du Temps* and *Farouche*. For Molinard, Lalique designed the presentation for *Calendal* and *Molinard*; the bottle for the latter was originally designed in 1929 for *Les Iscles d'Or*. Baccarat also designed for Molinard, creating *Xmas Bells* and *1811*.

Verreries Brosse brought us the frosted Art Deco beauty of Lentheric's *Miracle* in 1936, and bottles far too innumerable to mention for other industry giants since the mid-19th century.

Others have achieved legendary status as independent artists in the field. Pierre Dinand, for one, designed Balenciaga's *Prelude*, Balmain's *Ivoire*, Caron's *Nocturnes* and *Eau de Caron*, Givenchy's *Ysatis*, Guy LaRoche's *Drakkar Noir*, Paco Rabanne's *Calandre*, Pierre Cardin's *Cardin*, and Yves Saint Laurent's *Opium*, among others.

Jean Helleu was behind the cobalt blue beauty of *Evening in Paris*. The *Moss Rose* design for Charles of the Ritz was the work of Lawrence Colwell.

Armand Rateu envisioned the beauty that became Lanvin's elegant 1927 black and gold bottle for *Arpege*. Paul Iribe, who also created the *My Sin* bottle for the same company, is responsible for the Lanvin emblem, adapted from a portrait of Jeanne Lanvin and her daughter. In a departure from the usual crystal and glass, Leon Leyritz worked in procelain, designing Jean Desprez' *Grand Dame* in 1939 and *Bal d' Versaille* in 1969.

Felice Bergaud is credited with a host of Caron offerings, including *Fleurs de Rocaille*; Felicie Vanpouille was responsible for Caron's *Bellodgia*; Jacques Bocquet designed *Ma Griffe* and *Vetiver*. Serge Mansau, a French sculptor, is responsible for Christian Dior's *Diorella*, Caron's *Infini*, Oscar de la Renta's *Oscar de la Renta*, Revillon's *Detchema*, and Sonia Rykiel's *Septieme Sens*, among others.

Susan Wacker, design director for Elizabeth Arden, created the glorious, award-winning bottle for Elizabeth Taylor's *White Diamonds*. In what surely qualifies as a "fragrance family affair," the elegant bottle for *Donna Karan, New York* was designed by sculptor Stephen Weiss, Ms. Karan's husband.

Another American designer, Marc Rosen, a graduate of Carnegie Mellon and the Pratt Institute, has made his own substantial contribution to the art of innovative bottle design with such classic beauties as *Lagerfeld*, *KL*, *Jontue*, *Fendi*, *Red Door*, *Catalyst* and the more recent *Dahlia*, in honor of his wife, actress Arlene Dahl.

Collectively and individually, these artists represent many others from the past and present who all deserve our heartfelt admiration. Each has given credence to the expression "a feast for the eyes" with a host of classic perfume bottles that are capable of producing a gamut of emotions, from awe to delight to amusement. Without their genius and ingenuity, perfumes would merely be "splendid scents in mediocre bottles," just like the ones from which Francois Coty rescued Victorian ladies so many years ago!

The Creators

There would, however, have been no early entrepreneurs, no couturier scents, no fragrance companies, cosmetic companies, department stores' perfume counters or pharmaceutical house perfume branches without the skill of those who created the actual scents that have pleasured the senses of generations. Many of these olfactory artists were the companies' founders, who painstakingly blended their own fragrances. Some were those members of the founder's family lucky enough to be blessed with "a nose" as well, like the offspring of Francoise Coty and Guerlain. But

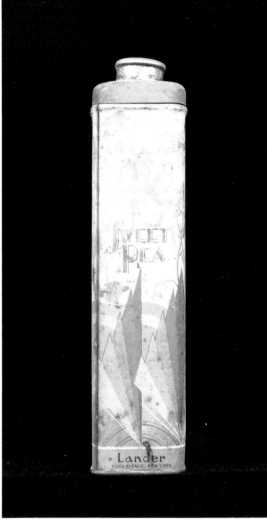

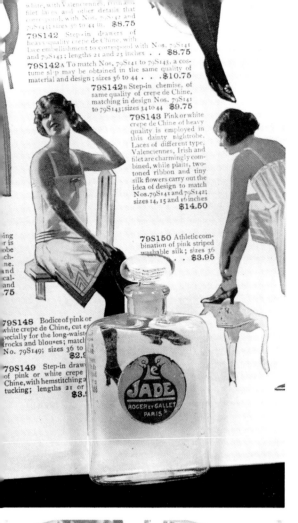

others, too innumerable to mention, have also honed the intricacies of combining just the right ingredients in just the right proportions.

Much like the unending combinations of musical notes that magically produce melodies throughout eternity, so too do intricate combinations of ingredients enable the art of perfume to be carried ever forward–but not without that very special "fragrance musician." Like many a great painter, violinist, or pianist, their expertise is perhaps a talent inborn. Whatever the answer–a secret to which we will probably never be privy–without these gifted individuals there would be no perfume industry at all!

It is a massive yet delicate undertaking that transports a scent from the laboratory where it is conceived to the drawing boards of the bottle designers. Whether it be a renowned house of fragrance, an illustrious couturier, a pharmaceutical or cosmetic empire, a retailing giant, or that old-time apothecary of Francois Coty's day, each has played its own role in the parade of new and exciting fragrances that have for decades appeared with remarkable consistency on perfume counters and thence to boudoirs and dressing tables.

With such luminaries lighting the way, it appears unlikely that women of this or future generations will ever be without a bounty of new offerings to "whet the senses." Rest assured that avid collectors–and even the merely sentimental–will continue to experience the thrill of uncovering new and exciting bottles ad infinitum!

[1,2,3] "The Art of Fashion Accessories," p. 67.

BIBLIOGRAPHY

Ball, Joanne Dubbs and Torem, Dorothy Hehl, *The Art of Fashion Accessories*, Schiffer Publishing Ltd., Exton, PA, 1993.

Dohanian, Phyllis, "Collector's Choice Award," *Perfume and Scent Bottle News*, vol. V, no. IV, Galena, Ohio.

Gaborit, Jean-Yves, *Perfumes, The Essences and Their Bottles*, Rizzoli International Publishing, Inc., N.Y., 1985.

Jones-North, Jacqueline Y., *Commercial Perfume Bottles*, Schiffer Publishing Ltd., Exton, PA, 1987.

Mason, Frederick, "The Romance and History of Perfume," *The Mentor*, Crowell Publishing Co., Springfield, Ohio, December 1922.

Sparrow, Bonita, "Perfume Bottle Designer Marc Rosen Educates, Entertains at Annual Meeting,"*Perfume and Scent Bottle News*, vol. V, no. IV, Galena, Ohio.

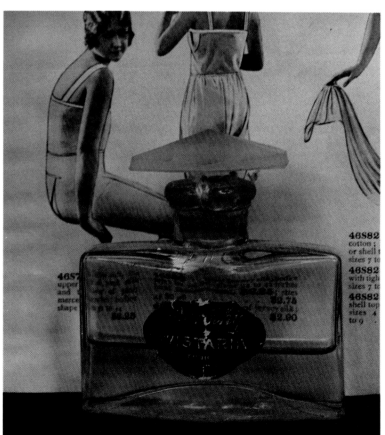

Section Two –
The Art of Perfume:
Its Romance and History

In one form or another, perfume has been with us throughout recorded history. The power of a pleasant fragrance was recognized early as a potent force for personal enhancement...or, frequently, to mask that which was unpleasant.

Like the limitless vagaries of other aspects of fashion, perfume was not used by the female sex alone. Male "dandies," who made liberal and creative use of scent, have existed in every century and in nearly every culture. They include the infamous fifteenth century gangs of Venetian hooligans who carried scented pomaders in a vain but valiant attempt to overcome the odors emanating from the canals' fetid waters. Farther west paraded the dapper British Macaronis a century later, affecting all manners of foppery–including carrying nosegays and wearing other outlandish accessories intended to startle the staid aristocracy. And finally, scent was put to good use by George "Beau" Brummell, the gentleman who made the term "dandy" more acceptable in polite society. As did many of their more conservative peers, all used fragrance–some to excess, others within the realm of good taste.

The mystique of perfume began long before this, however. Ancient Egyptians were well-versed in the secrets of scent, and the Bible is filled with mention of unguents and balms, frankincense, myrrh, and other perfumed oils. In the Far East, valuable spices were treasured not just for their use in uplifting the pleasures of food but also for their power to "uplift" the scents that had already become an integral part of the daily life of many of the world's civilizations. Even members of societies considered "barbarous" in the primitive world made use of fragrance to enhance personal allure.

By the time of the "flowering" of Greece, floral fragrances and aromatic plants like thyme and marjoram were highly popular. The austere Romans, too, considered perfume a necessary part of the toilette for both sexes. With the Roman conquest– first of Greece, and later of Mesopotamia, Turkey, Gaul (France), and the British Isles–came a greater consolidation of perfumery knowledge and skills. As the Empire ransacked the far places of the earth, it exposed the increasingly luxurious Romans to new and exciting foreign perfumes.

Frederick Mason, the author of a 1922 article in *The Mentor* on the history of perfume, noted that the Roman aristocracy "had a different scent for different parts of the body: mint for the arms, palm oil for the jaws and heart, marjoram for the eyebrows and hair, ground ivy essence for the knees and neck." Perfume became such a large part of their lifestyle, he wrote, that "a guild of perfumers–the 'Ungunetarii'–arose, and a whole street in Capua, one of the most important seaports, was given over to them."[1]

Even the emperors of Rome were susceptible to the temptations of scent. History records that Caligula, the ruler who built the famous Roman baths, excessively doused himself in perfume. For one festival, Nero spent four million sesterces (about $200,000) on roses. One record reports that "more perfume was consumed at the funeral of Emperor Nero's wife...than was sent from Arabia in a year."[2]

In the play "Antony and Cleopatra," notes Mason, Shakespeare has the Egyptian Cleopatra sailing down the River Cydnus to meet the Roman Mark Antony in a barge with sails "so perfumed that the winds were lovesick with them"[3]–a fitting scene for lovers from two ancient cultures whose histories are so thoroughly doused with wonderful fragrances.

The pall of the Dark Ages ushered in a dark age for perfumerie, and for the most part, the use of perfumes was limited to the Orient. The Crusades, however, once again gave Europe a "better scent," as hoardes of knights returned with rare perfumes for their lady loves. Nevertheless, Renaissance Italy must be given credit for yet another renaissance–the rebirth of fragrances. As Mason noted,

> For years Italy led in perfuming; it supplied the rest of Europe with sweet bags, perfume cakes for throwing on fires, fragrant candles and cosmetics, scented gloves and pomanders. The kings of France, however, drew the Italian masters to Paris with concessions and patronage, and soon France was started on its way to supremacy. Single scents no longer sufficed; perfumes were blended

Peep o' Day; Bean & Vail; 4"; 1885.

Caprice, "Extract for the Handkerchief," Colgate & Co. , N. Y. , handblown 2-1/4" bottle, cork stopper; introduced in 1883.

Lavender; Yardley; 4-1/4"; 1894.

De Bara Dusting Powder; American Products Co., Cincinnati; 4-1/2"; 1917.

to produce true bouquets. The chemist came to the aid of the perfumer and uncovered new sources of fragrance. Flower farms were established in regions of favorable climate, principally in a strip of Mediterranean coastline, from Marseilles to Genoa, and in the southern part of France, in the neighborhood of Grasse, Cannes, Nice, and Monaco.[4]

It was here, in France, that the use of fragrance was most widespread and luxurious–even Napoleon was reputed to have religiously doused himself with cologne, liberally bathing his shoulders and head with it in preparation for the rigors of each military campaign! Not to be outdone, Josephine chose musk as her favorite scent, with an odor so penetrating that neither washing with soap and water nor repainting could totally eliminate it from the palace walls. In the book *Memories of Saint Helena*, Victor Masson records that as Napoleon I lay dying, "two of Houbigant's perfumed pastilles were burning in his room."[5]

Napoleon and his Empress were, of course, mimicked by others of the French Court, which was by that time rife with scents–and nonsense! Few outdid the obsessive Madame de Pompadour, however, who so depended on the seductive power of fragrance that she was rumored to have spent nearly a million francs each year on perfumes.

Many substances used as bases for perfumes have strange animal origins: musk from the musk deer; ambergris, a secretion from the sperm whale; civet, from the Oriental cat of the same name; castor, from the beaver. But the most interesting process of the perfumer's art is that associated with the cultivation of flowers, like Parma violets, jonquils, orange blossoms, roses, lilies, jasmine, heliotrope, carnations, geraniums–all abloom in fields of seemingly unending color. Under ideal conditions, perfume-makers pick each blossom at the peak of its strength. This time varies greatly between the different species of flowers, and for some is as specific a period as a given number of hours after exposure to the sun.

Mason left little doubt as to the enormity of this magical transformation from flowers to perfume when he reported,

> In one parfumerie alone, in one year, the following flowers were used: 2,400 tons of roses, 1,750 tons of orange blossoms, 132 tons of violets, 280 tons of jasmine, 70 tons of tuberoses, 15 tons of jonquils. These are not so impressive when on realizes that 11 tons of roses–about 3,000,000 blossoms–are required to make one pound of attar of roses.[6]

But sophisticated perfumes are not simple distillations of great quantities of flowers. Mason also wrote about an English authority on perfumes, Septimus Piesse, who attempted to show that a scale exists among odors as among sound. Piesse "arranged them as in music, the sharp smells as the high notes, the heavier ones as the low. He held that in blending odors the same harmony should prevail as in music; that a false odor would have the same effect as a false note in a musical chord." Piesse termed his scale of smells an "odophone."[7]

The richest of perfumes are complex blends of many scents. A masterful knowledge of the many ingredients and insightful understanding of how each interacts with the others is required to create a distinctive fragrance.

Without a doubt, the choices of perfumes presented to modern women are staggering–but women (and men) need not be overwhelmed. It may be helpful for perfume connoisseurs and novices alike to follow Mason's 1922 advice: "Women had best rely upon instinct to guide them in their choice; it serves the woman of today, with a thousand scents to choose from, as unerringly as it served the woman of Egypt, who had but few."[8]

More than seventy years later, his words still ring true!

[1] "The Romance and History of Perfume," *The Mentor*, p. 3.
[2] "The Romance and History of Perfume," *The Mentor*, pp. 5-6.
[3] "The Romance and History of Perfume," *The Mentor*, p. 7.
[4] "The Romance and History of Perfume," *The Mentor*, p. 3.
[5] "Perfumes, the Essences and Their Bottles," Jean Yves Gaborit, p. 68.
[6] "The Romance and History of Perfume," *The Mentor*, p. 3.
[7] "The Romance and History of Perfume," *The Mentor*, p. 3.
[8] "The Romance and History of Perfume," *The Mentor*, p. 7.

Veritable; Guerlain; 6"; 1875.

Heliotrope; Colgate & Co.

An early treasure! *Caprice de la Mode;* Paul Prot & Co. , Successeur, Paris France; Lubin Perfumer, Perfumers of Paris, Russia & England; Rue St. Ann; marked HP on bottom (representative marking of the French glassworks of Pochet et du Courval)

Jockey Club; manufactured expressly for Knox & Charlton, an apothecary or emporium in Fall River, Mass.

Triple Extract; Jules Carnot & Cie, Paris; turn of century.

Jean Marie Farina, 2-3/4", Roger et Gallet; late 1800s, early 1900s.

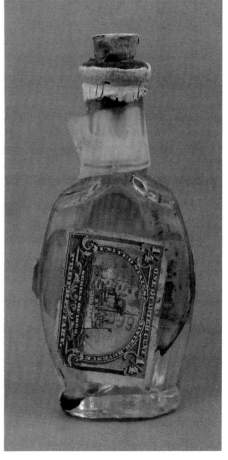

Front and back of *Royal White Rose*; Eastman; late 1800s.

Wisteria perfume, *Cashmere Bouquet* toilet water and soap; Colgate & Co., late 19th to early 20th centuries.

Fleur de Marie Handkerchief Extract, 2-1/2", cork stopper; Adolph Spiehler, Rochester, N. Y.; late 1800s, early 1900s.

Infusion; Ybry; 6" x 2-1/4"; cork stopper; early 20th century.

Pearls of Lilies; Wm. H. Brown, Baltimore; early cork-stoppered bottle.

An early offering of *Cologne Water*; Caswell Massey; 3-3/4" probably 1800s.

This 2" Limoges bottle from the turn of the century held an unknown fragrance.

Farina Cologne; Chas. B. Rogers & Co; 3-1/2"; turn of century or earlier.

White Rose and *Jockey Club*; 3-1/2"
bottles in 7" x 4" casque of mustard
gold velour, lined in gold raw silk;
Caswell Massey; early 1900s.

NEW YORK,
578 FIFTH AVE.
1121 BROADWAY,

NEWPORT, R. I.
6 CASINO BUILDING
167 THAMES ST.

Charmaine; early cork-stoppered bottle, black wooden top; 2-1/4", "7" on bottom. Unknown maker.

Unknown scent in early bottle marked L. Legrand, Parfumeur, Paris; 4-1/2". (L. Legrand company was founded in Paris in 1862.)

Monad Violet; Colgate & Co.; "W" on bottom of bottle; 1901.

Frangipanni; C. E. Nichols; 2-3/4"; early 1900s.

Rieger's California Perfume; Paul Rieger & Co., San Francisco; turn of century.

Eau D'Espagne; Roger & Gallet.

Trailing Arbutus; California Perfume Company.

Happy Holidays! *Xmas E*; Fragonard Grasse; cork stopper; early 20th century.

Wood Violet; Parfum Alberta, Art Nouveau label; 3-1/4"; early 1900s.

Azurea; L.T. Piver, Paris; turn of the century.

From early in the century, Vantine's presentation case holds everything to keep milady beautiful: India Pearl Tooth Powder, *Wisteria Blossom* Cologne, Kritch Sandalwood Talcum and Extract, and lip gloss.

Violet Sec; one of Richard Hudnut's earliest; 1896.

Three Flowers; Richard Hudnut; 1915.

White Heliotrope; early Richard Hudnut.

Violet Sec Toilet Water; Richard Hudnut.

Narcissus; Jergens; 1-1/4"; early 20th century.

Jasmin Fascinato; Carlova; 3" x 2-1/2"; cork stopper; early 20th century.

3-1/4" unmarked iridescent bottle, blown glass stopper.

Le Prince; 1-5/8", "Sixteen 129" on bottom; no maker; early 1900s.

Select Violet; Gordon & Co. , cork stopper; turn of century.

These early unidentified scents by Coty and F. Millot have stoppers of similar design.

4-1/2" unmarked bottle, acid marked France P. V.

Mouson Lavendel; Mit der Postkutche.

Violet Simplicity; flowers and bows with a frosted stopper; Wm. H. Brown & Bro. Co., Baltimore; 1900.

American Beauty Rose; 4"; Larkin & Co., Buffalo, N.Y.; "Leo" on stopper; early 1900s.

An array of products from Richard Hudnut's *Three Flowers*.

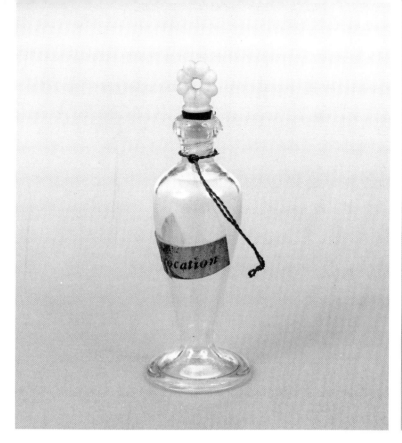

My Avocation;   5-1/8" bottle, ivory
floral stopper; early 1900s.

Extract de Violette de Parme, 3-1/2",
Roger et Gallet, N. Y. , Paris; late
1800s, early 1900s.

A selection of *Orange Blossom* toiletries.

Lilac Sweets trade card; Solon Palmer.

A staple of every boudoir in Victorian times: smelling salts from the local apothecary.

White Heliotrope; 3-1/2"; Solon Palmer.

Dactylis; Colgate & Co.; 1-1/2", "W"
on bottom; 1901.

Azurea Poudre et Sachet; L.T. Piver,
Paris and New York, made in France;
box reads "Poudre de Riz, Safronor,
Blanche" on bottom; 1907.

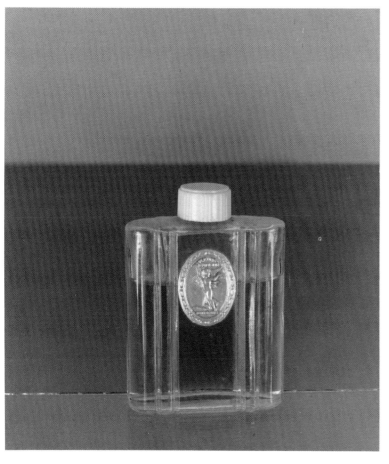

Fleur d' Amour; Roger et Gallet;
2-1/2" x 2" hand-blown bottle,
marked "M" on bottom; 1902.

Fleurs de Amour talc; Roger et Gallet;
1902.

The enduring and angelic classic *Djer Kiss* Parfum and Sachet by Kerkoff; 1908.

Rusalka Talcum; Otis Clapp & Son; 1909.

Oeillet Fane; Grenoville, Paris; 1910.

Ambre; D'Orsay; Lalique bottle; introduced in teens. Photo courtesy of Annie Bower.

Chevalier; D'Orsay; 1912.

Mystere; D'Orsay; Lalique bottle from 1920s; fragrance introduced in 1915. Photo courtesy of Annie Bower.

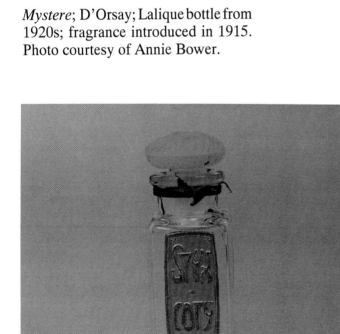

Styx; Coty; 2" Lalique bottle; introduced 1912.

Lily of the Valley; Colgate & Co., N.Y.; 2-1/2"; early 1900s.

Un Air Embaume; Rigaud; 4-1/2";
1915.

Mavis; Vivadou; 1915.

Advertisement for *Mary Garden
Perfume,* Rigaud, April, 1917.

Goyesca; Myrurgia, Barcelona, Spain; 1919.

De Bara powder; American Products Co.; 1917. F.R. Lazarus Smelling Salts; turn of the century. *Sachet*; Harriet Hubbard Ayer; 1920s.

Advertisement for *Rose Real Beauty*, Marinello Toilet Preparations, April 1917.

Unlabelled decanter-style bottle for *Le Vertige*; Coty; 4"; acid-marked "923iii." This presentation probably dates from the 1920s.

Paris de Coty; 5"; bottle acid-marked
"5" on bottom; introduced in 1921.

Advertisement for *Un Air Embaume,*
Regaud, 1920.

April Showers; Cheramy, France; 2";
introduced 1921.

Gardenia; Duchess of Paris; 2".

Gemey; Richard Hudnut; 2-1/4";
marked "171" on bottom; introduced
in 1923.

Toujours Moi; 2-1/2"; Corday, Paris; "Corday, French bottle" on bottom; introduced in 1923.

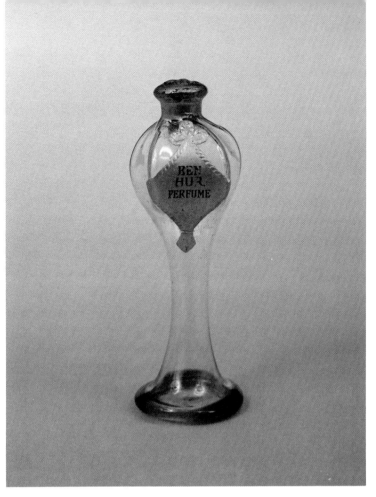

Ben Hur Perfume; 2-3/8" hand blown bottle; manufacturer unknown.

AS ≈ THE ≈ PETALS

THE only "right" face powder is the one that improves your appearance and your complexion at the same time!

Try *As-the-Petals*—it protects, improves and beautifies! The secret is in its medicinal properties which help banish the worry of a rough, red, sallow or shiny skin!

Besides the Face Powder, which is 60c, there is *As-the-Petals* Rouge, in metal box with mirror and puff, at 50c. Other *As-the-Petals* toilet requisites are the Talcum Powder at 25c, Extract at $1.50, Toilet Water at $1.50 and Sachet at 75c.

Crème de Meridor, the original greaseless cream, is the ideal foundation for *As-the-Petals* Face Powder. For all occasions and seasons—a day and night cream in one. 25c and 50c jars.

Lazell PERFUMER
Dept. 2-E, Newburgh-on-the-Hudson
New York

Send for free samples of *As-the-Petals* Face Powder and *Crème de Meridor*. For 25c in stamps we will also send a bottle of bewitching *As-the-Petals* Perfume.

As the Petals, Lazell Perfumer, 1920.

Unlabelled bottle of slag marble; 4-1/2"; marked "Renaud, Paris 1817, made in Paris, Pat. Pend.;" probably 1920s.

Chanel No. 5 in classic Chanel bottle; introduced in 1921.

Boldoot Imperial boxed set; J. C. Boldoot, Amersterdam, Netherlands; introduced in 1925, continued to be marketed into the 1950s.

Shalimar; Guerlain; 5-3/4" x 4" bottle in 8-1/4" x 5-1/2" purple velour presentation case. This classic Shalimar bottle was designed by Raymond Guerlain and manufactured by Baccarat in 1927. The name Shalimar literally means "abode of love" and was inspired by Mumtaz Mahal, for whom Shah Jehan built the Taj Mahal.

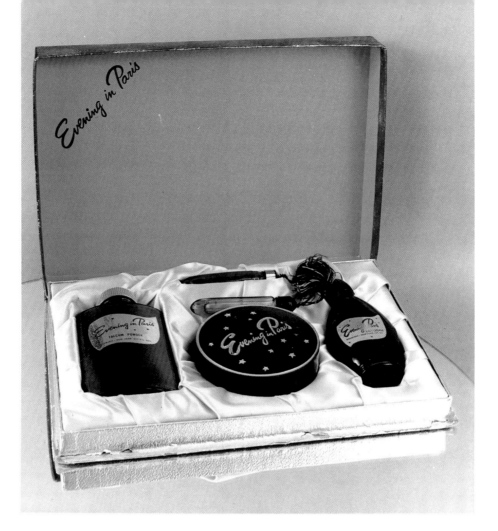

Evening in Paris; Bourjois; boxed set, consisting of talc, cologne, powder and perfume vials; the powder box has a metal top instead of the standard heavy cardboard container found later. Introduced in 1929, *Evening in Paris* reached the peak of its popularity in the 1940s. The now classic cobalt bottle was designed by Jean Helleu and manufactured by Verreries Brosse.

Evening in Paris; 3" perfume vial.

Muguet Des Bois; Coty; 2-1/8", Lalique designer label; introduced 1923.

A world-renowned classic, *Bellodgia* by Caron. The bottle was designed by Caron co-owner Felicie Vanpouille in 1927.

Nuit de Noel; Caron; 4-1/4" x 2-1/2"; 1922.

Nuit de Noel; Caron; Shagreen box with giant tassel; 1922.

Lucretia Vanderbilt perfume (McKesson & Robbins), with trademark butterfly-designed compact; late 1920s.

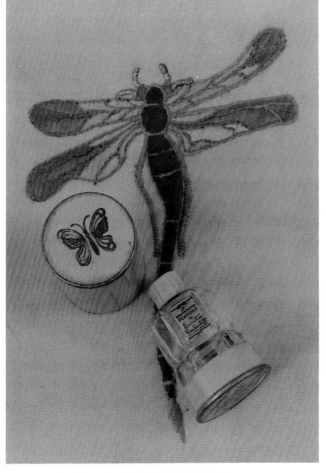

Mitsouoko; Guerlain, introduced in Paris in 1919, in U.S. in 1922. 4-3/4" Lalique-type frosted bottle; marked "30," made in France. Named for the heroine in *Madame Butterfly*, it was originally presented in the same Baccarat bottle as *L'Heure Bleue*.

Lucretia Vanderbilt (N. Y.), A Concentrated Perfume; McKesson & Robbins; 1-3/4"; interlocking eliptical marks with "3" and "7" on either side on the bottom.

Three Flowers; Richard Hudnut; 3"; 1920s.

Chypre; L. T. Piver; Persian influence on label and box; 3".

Fit for a Prince: *Princess Charming*; from Harriet Hubbard Ayer, a companion to 1922's *Prince Charming*.

Crepe de Chine; F. Millot; 1929.

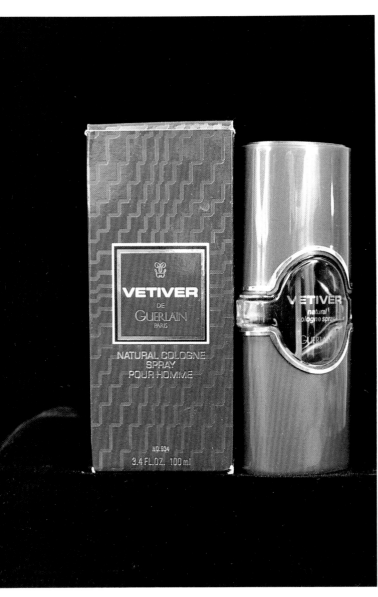

Vetiver; Guerlain; early 1920s.

Rubyat; another Persian-inspired perfume.

Le Dandy; D'Orsay; 1926.

D'Orsay of Paris advertisement, 1920.

Blue Waltz; Joubert; 2-3/4"; 1927.

White Rose; Adolph Spiehler; 3-1/2";
1920s.

Ave Maria; Prince Matchabelli; 1-3/4"
x 1-1/2"; 1926.

Renaud slag bottle; unknown scent;
1-1/2" x 1-3/4"; probably late 1920s or
Thirties.

No. 22; Chanel; 2-3/8"; bottom marked
"Chanel 17 France"; 1922.

CHANEL GARDENIA
Chanel captures the true fragrance
of those fragile blossoms to give
you glamour, youthful delicacy . . . a
perfume ever reminiscent of spring.

CHANEL

Black Gardenia; Chanel; 2-1/2" in beige suede snap-top case; 1921.

Miracle; Lentheric; 3"; 1924.

In step with the times: early *Emeraude*; Persian-inspired bottles and powder box; Coty; 1923.

Sweet Pea; Duvinne; 2-1/4"; 1926. Probably part of a floral series by Duvinne, which also included *Jasmin* and *Narcissus.*

Liu; Guerlain; 2-3/8"; named for character in Puccini's opera *Turandot*; 1929.

Mitcham Lavender; Potter & Moore. *Mitcham* was introduced by Potter & Moore in 1888; this presentation of *Lavender* was probably from the 1920s or Thirties.

The cool beauty of white and gold...*L'Origan* (5") by Coty; D'Anjou's *Jasmin* and *Ideal* .

Arpege; Lanvin; 2-3/4"; introduced in 1927; bottle current.

TiJade; D'Arline by American Druggists Syndicate; floral Lalique-style frosted stopper; 2" x 2-1/4"; black leaf box; 1923.

Sweet Pea...Flowers of the Morning; House of Martens, N.Y.

Mon   Boudoir, Houbigant, 1922.

Mysteries of the Orient marked *Tzigana;* unknown maker; probably 1920s.

Toujours Moi, Corday.

Rose Nouvelle; Miro Dena; Paris; 5" x 3-1/2"; 1920s.

Narcisse; Loubenne; 1-1/2".

Amour Sauvage; Ybry; 1-1/2"; 1929.

Preciosa; Pinaud; aqua velour presentation case.

L'Heure Bleue Eau de Toilette de Guerlain; 6-1/2" x 4".

Bois Dormant; Houbigant; 1-3/4";
1925.

Lilas Royal; Lubin; 2-1/2".

Jockey Club; Riker-Hegemen; 2-1/4".
Riker-Hegeman created fragrances
early in the century; this one is most
likely from the 1920s.

Balai; unknown maker; 3".

Muguet des Bois; Coty; 4"; 1923.

La Vierge Folle; Poiret Perfume Co.

Crepe De Chine; F. Millot; 1929.

Southern France Face Powder; unknown maker.

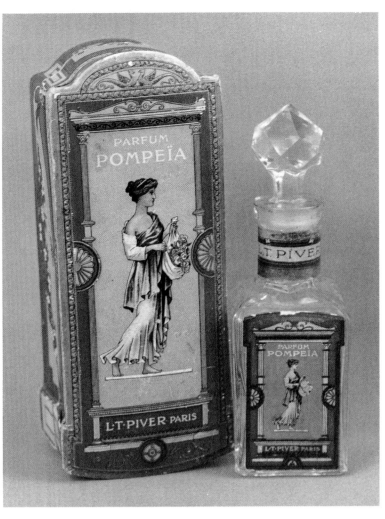

Parfum Pompeia; L.T. Piver, Paris;
4-1/2"; 1922.

Gardenia; Valois; 3".

Jasmin; Fioret; 2-3/4"; 1920s.

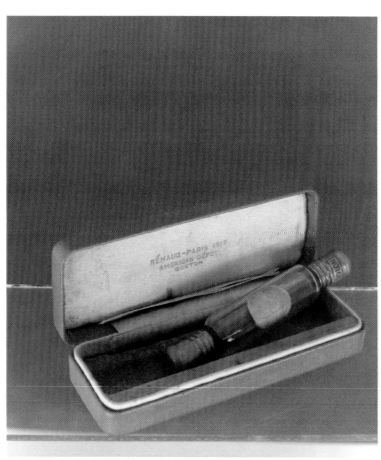

Muguet des Bois; Coty; 2-1/8"; 1923.

Notchenka liquid lip color; Renaud;
2-3/4" vial in pink leather case; 1920s.

Venetian Dusting Powder; Elizabeth
Arden; 1920s.

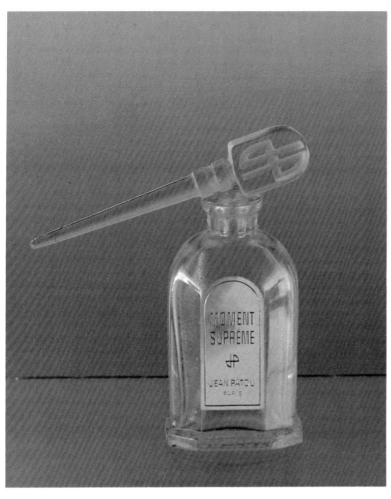

Moment Supreme; Patou; 3"; 1929.

L'Aimant; Coty; 4-3/4"; Red Bakelite top; 1927.

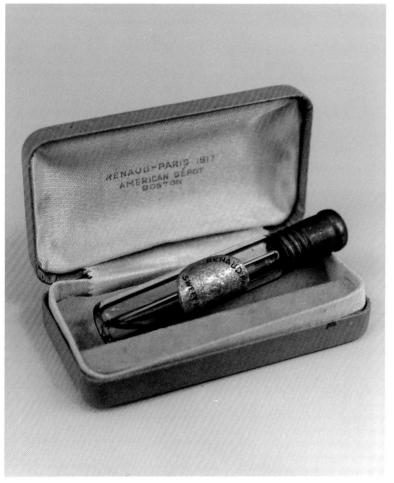

Sweet Pea; Renaud; 1920s.

Cappi Dusting Powder; Cheramy.

Guerlain Talcum —

fragrance that

clings

and soothes at the same time.

The incredibly silky powder

is scented with a sachet-strength

of Shalimar, L'Heure Bleue, Liu,

Vol de Nuit, Mitsouko or

Fleur de Feu. 2.00 plus Fed. tax.

The talcum for Guerlain's premier scents remained popular for decades after their first release, as seen in this 1940s advertisement. Courtesy of Lord & Taylor.

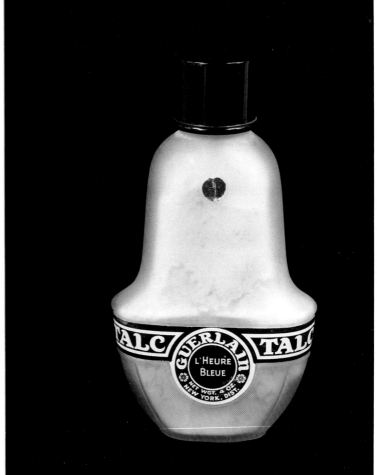

L'Heure Bleue Talc; Guerlain; 5-3/4".

Tandem set by Coty held black leather snap-top case, cylindrical metal parfum holders and a vial of Coty's *Paris. Tandem* was introduced by Coty in 1927, *Paris* in 1921.

Evening in Paris Talcum Powder;
Bourjois.

Narcisse; Richard Hudnut.

Acaciosa; Caron; 7-1/4"; 1923.

Petalia; Tokalon, Paris; powder box
companion to the perfume bottle designed by R. Lalique; 1925.

Front and back of *Bouquet* by Annette.

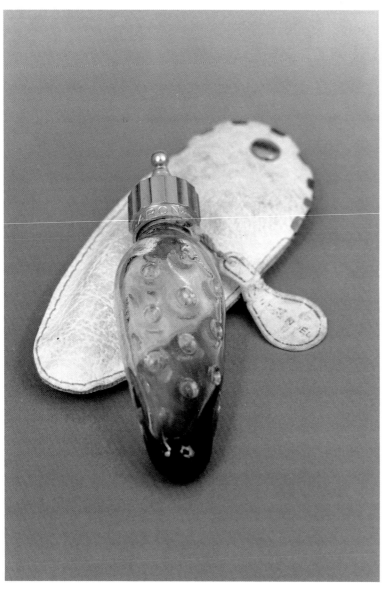

Nuit de Noel; Caron; white leather holder; 1922.

Lotion Vegetale Mitsouko; Guerlain.

A Coty trio...*Styx*; 1912 (the large and the small of it) flank *L'Aimant*; 1927.

Fidelwood; 2"; House of Bermuda.

La Saison des Fleurs; Lionceau; 1925; top slides open to reveal ivory die, which in turn open to reveal perfumed pomader inside.

Early bottles with ornate metal daubers; unknown scent and maker.

An unusual hexagonal talcum powder
tin has a "peek" into milady's boudoir
on lid and "sporting scenes" on each
side panel; unknown maker.

Gardenia; Richard Hudnut; charming boxed set, featuring toilet water, talcum, face powder, and cologne.

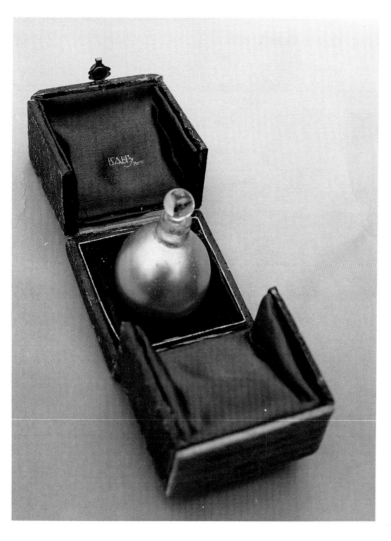

La Perle d'Isabey; Isabey; 1920s.

Narcisse; Lander; frosted Deco-style top.

Brilliantine; Blue Waltz (Joubert); 1927.

Violet Essence; Elizabeth Arden

Bluebell Eau de Toilette; Penhaligon, London (established in 1870); Photo by Robert Ball.

L'Aimant; Coty.

Fete; Molyneaux; 1927.

This scent bottle sported its own chrome travel case. Photograph by Robert Ball.

This 7-3/4" Baccarat bottle housed Houbigant's *Quelques Fleurs* and *Parfum Ideal*; 1925. Photo courtesy of Annie Bower.

Le Jade, Roger et Gallet; introduced in 1923.

Friendship's Garden, Shulton, 3½.
Introduced in 1939

 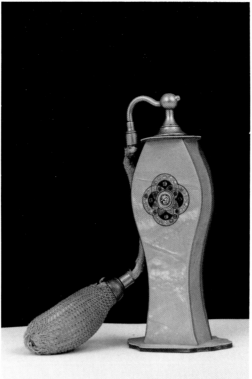 

Madisha; 1-1/2"; 31 on bottom; St. Sauveur, France.

Celluloid bottle, indicative of the 1930s; no label, 5-1/2".

Winky; 1-3/8" bottle; marked "S.GD 20" on bottom; St. Sauveur, France.

Frou Frou du Gardenia; Dunhill; 2-1/2".

Chypre, L'Origan, Styx; Coty advertisement from 1930 issue of L'Illustration .

Indiscret; Lucien Lelong; 1-3/4"; introduced in 1935.

Sortilege; Le Galion; 2"; introduced 1937.

Desirable; 2-1/4", Luzier, Inc.

Green glass bottle; 3"; no label; marked
Czechoslovakia.

B. Altman, New York, advertisement
from December 1930.

French CanCan; Caron; 2-1/2"; 1936.

Deviltry; De Raymond; 3-1/2" bottle
marked Czechoslovakia; introduced
1936.

Cuir de Russie; De Trevisse, Paris; 2-1/2".

4-3/4" handpainted bottle, no label.

Khus Khus; 3-1/2", Solomon's Triple Extract, Kingston, Jamaica.

d'Esterel; 2-1/2", made in France, interlocking VR on bottom, but without maker name.

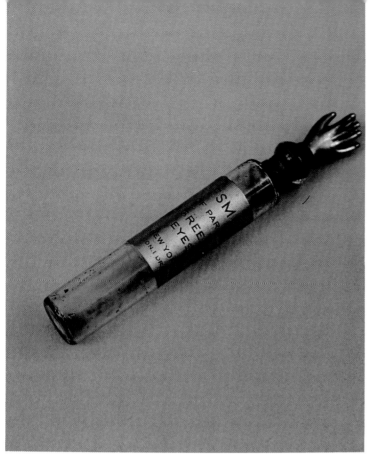

Green Eyes; Esme; 3-1/8" (1 dram); unusual cork stopper with pewter-like hand.

Chance; Cherigan (Cuba); 1-3/4"; introduced 1937.

Danger; Ciro; 3"; introduced 1938.

Fleurs d' Ete; Bienaime, Paris; 3-5/8" bottle marked "made in France"; introduced 1935.

Marie Antoinette; Liatris, Paris; 3".

Nosegay;   Dorothy Gray;   2"; introduced 1938.

Shanghai; Lentheric; 2".

Apple Blossom; Helena Rubenstein; 1-1/2".

Cherry Blossom cologne; D'Orsay; 4-1/2".

Muguet; Houbigant.

Shocking in famous flower-bedecked "dressmaker" design; Schiaparelli; 6" x 3" bottle in pink satin-lined presentation case; 1937.

Shocking; Schiaparelli; leather travel case; 1939.

Shocking Dusting Powder; Schiaparelli; 1936.

Gardenia (part of the "American Memories" series); Solon Palmer, N.Y.

Blue Grass; Elizabeth Arden; 3-3/4" French bottle; 1934.

Celui; Jean Desses; frosted bottle; 1938.

Dandy (men's fragrance); D'Orsay; 3"
x 2".

Under lock and key...a charming presentation by Cardinal.

Sortilege; LeGalion; 1937.

A floral delight...*A Bien Tot*; Lentheric;
5-1/4" x 3"; 1930.

Grrrrr...*Tigress*; Faberge; 2"; 1938.

"My heart has wings..." *Latitude 50* by Revillon; wing-shaped 3-1/2" x 3-1/2" bottle; 1935.

Aphrodisia; Faberge; 3-1/2"; 1932.

The classic *Tweed* by Lentheric; modernistic wooden top; lift top box; 3"; 1935. The same design held the earlier European version, called *Risque-Tout*

For the *Joy* of it!

Joy; Patou; jet black bottle with red
synthetic top; gold "logo" box; 1931.

Joy; Patou; black glass bottle with red,
gold sealed top, encased in its own
suede box; 1931.

Joy; Patou; satin and velour-lined gold
box; 1931.

Joy; Patou; 2" bottle in 3" box; 1931.

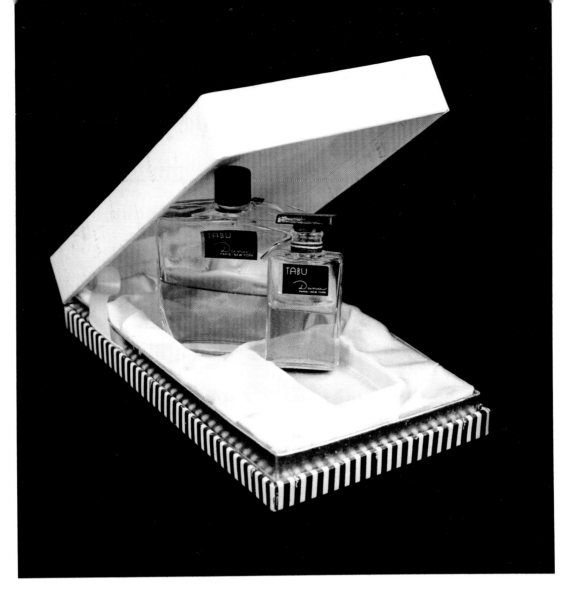

Tabu and "double" Tabu; Dana; two
sizes in lift-top presentation case; 1932.

Lily of the Valley; Le Galion.

Vega; Guerlain; 3" bottle marked
Baccarat.

Red hot heart, *Fleur de Rhodes*; unknown maker.

Sortilege; Le Galion.

With a gypsy influence, *Balalaika;* Lucien Lelong; 5"; 1939.

Under lock and key: *Gardenia, Chypre,* and *Bouquet* a three-bottle set by Cardinal in a 4-1/2" container.

Bouquet, Lilac, Gardenia; Mode Perfumes.

Gala Night; Bouton (Geo. M/. Bouton Co.).

The "blue butterfly," a charming mini from *Lucretia Vanderbilt.*

Miracle by Lentheric (front); 2-1/2"; *Countess Maritza* (left rear) by Paris Laboratories, 4-3/4" x 3", 1931; unidentified fragrance by Patou (right rear), 3-1/2" x 2".

Frosted Art Deco's finest....*Miracle*, by Lentheric; 1924; this design, by Verreries Brosse in 1936, replaced the original black and gold Baccarat bottle.

Cassandra; Weil; 2"; lift-top box; 1935.

Patrician Lavender; Germany (Dist. by Tamak, Inc.), 3-1/4".

Mai Oui; Bourjois; 1938.

Lys Bleu; Caspar et Cie; 3-1/2" x 2-1/2".

Je Reviens by Worth, in grey suede pouch, alongside latticed perfume holder for the purse, and a "chess piece" for an unidentified Mary Chess fragrance.

4711 and *Tosca;* both 4-1/2"; Glockengasse Cologne on Rhine, Cologne, Germany.

Le Numbero Cinq; Molyneux; 3"; grey suede lift-top outer box, marked Extrait No. 30.

Pink Clover; Harriet Hubbard Ayer;
1938.

Fleurs De Rocaille; Caron; 2-1/2" in
4-1/2" box; 1933.

This powder jar by an unknown maker
came in an elegant pink satin case.

Invitation; Patou; 3-1/8"; 1932.

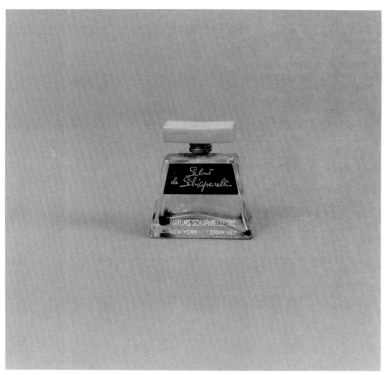

Salut; Schiaparelli; 1934.

Happiness Paul Jones, California; probably 1930s.

Salut; Schiaparelli; 6" x 3"; 1934.

Noir; Weil; 1930s.

Colony; Patou; 1937.

Marilyn Talc by Gibson-Howell Co. ,
Jersey City, N. J.

Le Moment Supreme; Poiret, Paris.

Heliotrope; California Perfume Co.

Mais Oui Talc; Bourjois; 1938.

Two beauties; a unique *Shalimar* bottle by Guerlain, teamed with an equally unusual *Je Reviens* offering by Worth.

Leather covered bottle, screw top; unknown scent and maker; 2".

Harmony Violet; Harmony.

Ecusson; Jean d'Albret; late 1940s or early 1950s.

Noel Joyeux; unknown maker; Catalin plastic case in the shape of a Christmas ornament holds mini bottle securely in place.

Baghari de Robert Piguet;   1-1/2";
France; introduced 1947.

Jolly, Eau Parfumee Parfums, 4" bottle acid-marked 6; Dinard, N.Y., 1940s.

Ma Griffe (my signature); Carven, Paris, France; 3" bottle with interlocking HP on bottom; bottle designed by Jacques Bocquet; 1945.

Sky Rocket; 3-3/4", Jean Pierre DuPont, New York, Paris.

FARNESIANA DE CARON

Advertisement for *Farnesiana de Caron;* from 1947 issue of *L'Illustration* .

White Shoulders; 3-1/2", Evyan, 1943.

Most Precious and *White Shoulders,*
2-1/2" gold hearts in presentation case;
Evyan, N. Y.; White Shoulders was
introduced in 1943, Most Precious in
1947.

Out of the water
with a splash—

White Shoulder's Splash, Evyan's light
fragrance that stimulates and scents
the whole body, keeps you refreshed
for hours. 3.00, 5.50, 10.00 plus tax.

Courtesy of Lord & Taylor.

Gallivanting Perfume, 2-1/2", Vita Ray, N. Y. , Division of Affiliated Products, Inc. , Jersey City, N. J. , 1940s.

Gallivanting Cologne, 4-3/4", Vita Ray, N. Y. , 1940s.

Beau Catcher; 4-7/8"; Vigny, 1940s.

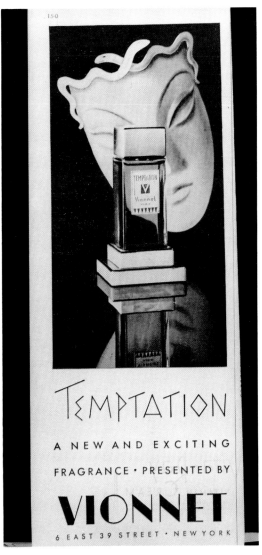

TEMPTATION

A NEW AND EXCITING

FRAGRANCE · PRESENTED BY

VIONNET

6 EAST 39 STREET · NEW YORK

Elaborate 3" x 2-1/4" cut glass bottle to grace any perfume lover's dressing table.

Bandit de Robert Piguet; introduced in 1944.

Following its introduction, a 1941 advertisement for *Dashing* by Lily Dache.

Primitif; by Max Factor; probably
1940s or Fifties.

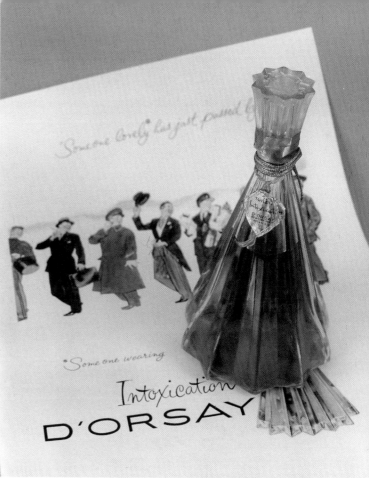

Intoxication; D'Orsay; 1942.

"The large and the small of it"...*Yanky
Clover* by Richard Hudnut; 1944.

And yet another *Yankee Clover*; 4-1/2"
x 1-1/2".

L'Origan boxed set with atomizer; Coty; this fragrance was introduced in 1909, but this was a mid-century presentation.

Advertisement for *L'Aimant* (The Magnet), Coty; from 1947 issue of *L'Illustration* .

Moss Rose by Charles of the Ritz; Cologne, Scented Balm, and Body Sachet in bottles designed by Lawrence Colwell in 1940. The tallest is 7-1/4".

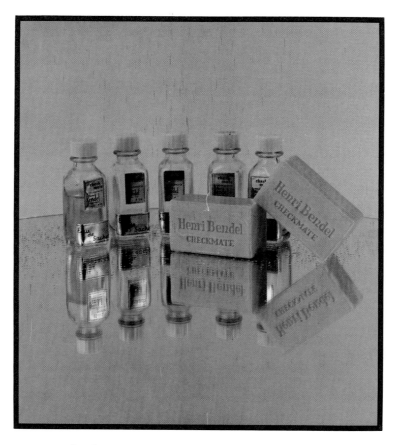

Checkmate; from boxed set of perfumes and soaps; Henri Bendel; 1942.

Miss Dior; Christian Dior; 3-1/2" x
3-1/4" frosted bottle, marked Christian
Dior, N.Y.; 1948.

L'Air du Temp; Nina Ricci; 1948.

Thou Shalt Not; Maupassant; 1944.

Magie; Lancome; 1949.

Tianne, 1-1/8" bottle, marked "2" on bottom; Nettie Rosenstein; introduced 1948.

Sissimo; Simonetta; 2-1/2" bottle with black velvet bow tie, marked "B" on bottom; post-war Italy.

No. 9; Leonid de Lescinskis, New York; 2"; 1944.

.... *Orgueil-the perfume that tells a woman she is chic... that she is lovely - and beloved*

Orgueil $10 $25 $110 *Perfume*

LUCIEN LELONG

A Lucien Lelong advertisement for *Orgueil,* introduced in 1946.

Tailspin; Lucien Lelong; 2-3/4"; 1940.

like the lingering memory of a never-forgotten symphony...Taglio, a new perfume by Lucien Lelong.

LUCIEN LELONG

A Lucien Lelong ad for *Taglio,* introduced in 1945.

For men, a giant bottle of *Snuff* by
Schiaparelli; 1940.

A 1940's advertisement for
Schiaparelli's *Shocking* .

This black suede pouch protected an
unknown scent by Worth.

Magie; Lancome; 2-3/4"; 1949.

A sophisticated presentation, no matter how hard the times! *Evening in Paris* goes to war. Underside of powder box reads "This is a temporary Victory package. The contents are unchanged."

A lovely scene with a lovely lady ready for a night on the town. Another *Evening in Paris* presentation by Boujois.

With a Glen Miller beat...*In the Mood*.

Evening Star; Blanchard; 2-5/8" purse size "traveler"; 1949

Femme; Marcel Rochas; 1945.

4-1/2" "accordian-pleated" bottle with fan top; unknown scent and maker.

Replique; Raphael; 1944.

Sandalwood; Roger & Gallet.

Golden Gardenia Exquisite; Lander;
1947.

Advertisement for *Ecarlate de Suzy,*
1947.

Le Dix; Balenciaga; 2-1/2"; 1947.

Le Dix; Balenciaga; 1947.

Ciro advertisement from early 1940s; note bottom reads: "And remember to buy War Bonds regularly."

Cara Nome Sachet; Langlois; 1940s.

A heart stopper...*Fleurs de Rhodes*;
unknown maker.

White Magnolia; Helena Rubenstein;
1949.

Marie Earle advertisement from a 1947
issue of *L'Illustration*.

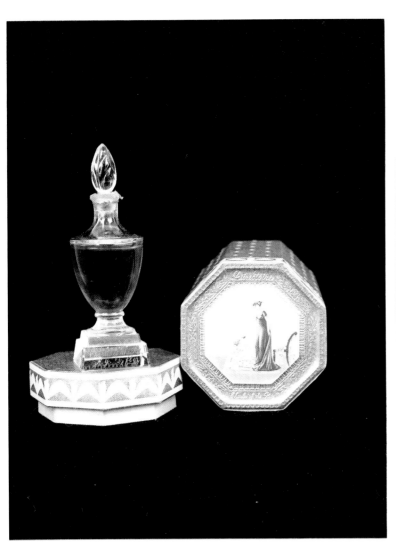

Directoire; Charles of the Ritz; 1945.

Divine; D'Orsay; 1940s.

A treasure trove...these 22K gold-washed figures held Hattie Carnegie's *49*; 1944; bottles by Wheaton.

They went thataway: *Desperado* men's cologne, in the same style bottle as *Balalaika*. Lucien Lelong, 2-3/4".

Shalimar advertisement, 1947.

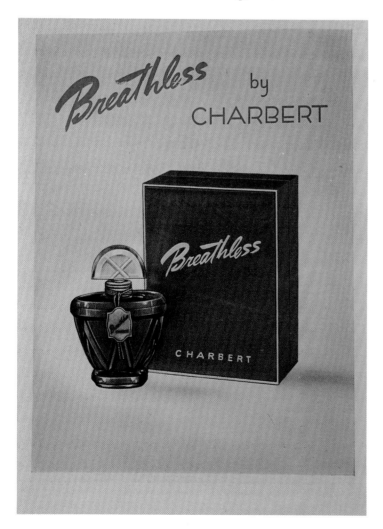

Charbert's *Breathless* in 1940's advertisement.

L'Heure Attendee; Patou; 3-bottle coffret; 1945.

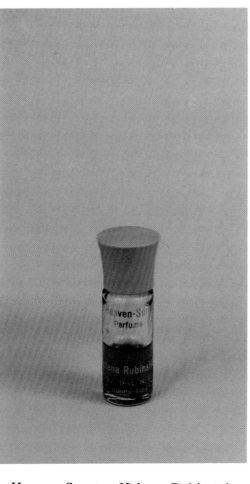

Tianne; Nettie Rosenstein; 1948.

Heaven Scent; Helena Rubinstein; 1941.

Startling Deco design by unknown maker; acrylic with aluminum top.

L'Air du Temps; Nina Ricci; 2"; 1948.

Soir de Montmarte; Paris; 1940s.

Coer de Joies; Lalique.

Hattie Carnegie Eau de Cologne in faux burlap box. Note the sealing wax to hold ribbon in place, and war-time Victory stamp at bottom left. Bottle is 5-1/4".

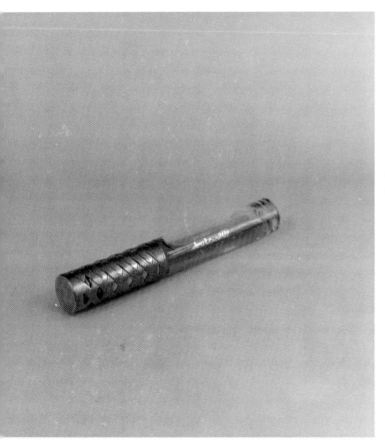

Fabregette; Faberge; purse-size vial in braided gold holder; 1947.

Oriental *Wisteria* by Kaya, Tokyo and New York; *Chinese Lotus*, unknown maker.

Odalisque; Nettie Rosenstein; frosted bottle; 1946.

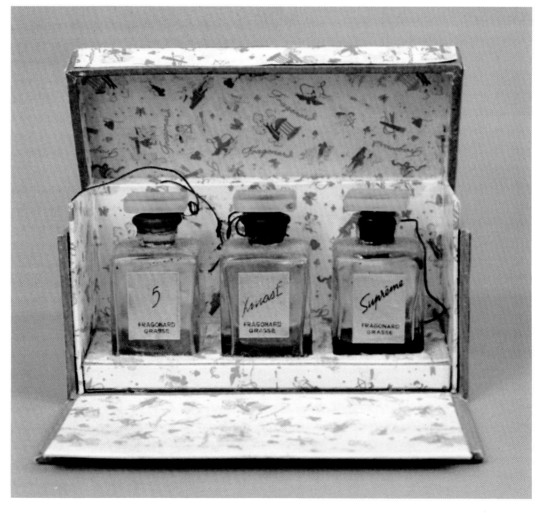

Boxed trio: 5, *Xmas E* and *Supreme*; Fragonard.

A checkered past...*Diorama*; Christian Dior; 1947.

Miss Dior; Christian Dior; 3-1/2" x 2-1/4"; 1948.

Unknown scent by Irresistible, New York.

Hobnail Cologne; Wrisley; 9 oz. milk glass bottle in classic "hobnail" design; 1940s.

Duchess of York; by Prince Matchabelli, 1930s.

Stradivari; 4" x 3" clear crown, Prince Matchabelli, 1940s.

In deviation from the standard Matchabelli crown, a giant 7" crystal bottle of *Wind Song*, marked "Collector's Edition"; 1953.

Potpourri; Matchabelli; 1940.

Delightful early scent bottles with novelty cork stoppers.

Picanette; Karoff; 1938.

A touch of whimsy; probably from the 1940s.

Golliwogs on parade; Vigny; 1919.

The form divine...unknown scent and maker; probably from the 1930s or '40s.

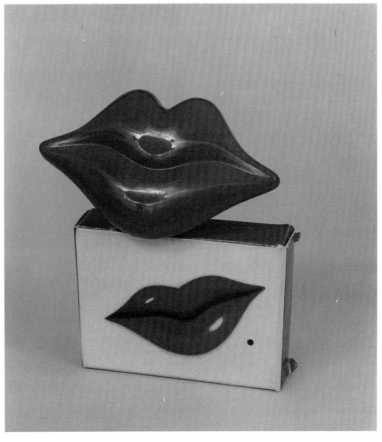

Pucker up! Avon lip gloss from the 1970s.

Brocade; Avon Products Co.; probably 1940s or Fifties.

Another clock by Avon; this one held an unknown scent, and was also most likely offered in the 1940s or Fifties.

"Tick tock" — unknown scent and maker; probably early 1900s.

Unlabeled bottle of whimsical "toilet" water, 1969.

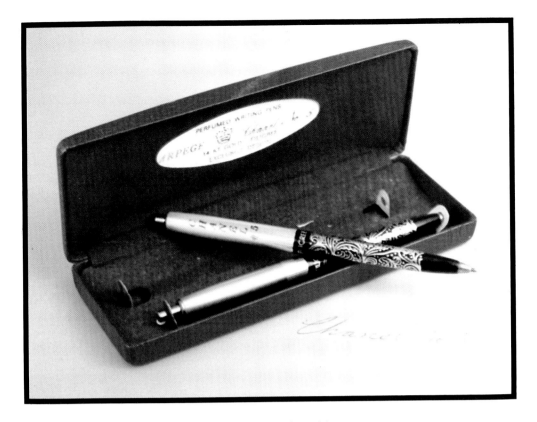

An unusual marketing idea — perfumed writing pens, one emitting the fragrance of *Chanel No. 5*, the other Lanvin's *Arpege*.

Around the World; Rose d'Or of Paris, Ltd.; celluloid container; bottles marked "Brazil, Sweden, Germany, Hawaii and Italy". Probably the 1950s or Sixties.

A 1940s novelty, this dime store *L'Orient* perfume by Laure was offered in a miniature "champagne" bottle.

This "Gentleman under glass" and his clown companion both held unknown scents and are of German porcelain.

Parfums *Rose Valois* feature three lovely ladies in their Spring chapeaus.

Happy Holidays from Cheramy; *April Showers* in a Christmas tree box. Although *April Showers* was introduced in 1921, this is probably from the 1930s or Forties.

Ring in the New Year! A giant 6-1/2" Christmas bell by Avon held *Crystalsong Sonnet* cologne; glass bell, lucite top and bow.

Novelty oil lamp with red shade; unknown fragrance and maker; 4".

All lit up! This 6-1/2" lamp with celluloid shade contained *Gardenia* by
Lander.

Gala Night, 2-1/2" bottle in 4-3/4"
hurricane lamp; Bouton.

The menagerie!

129

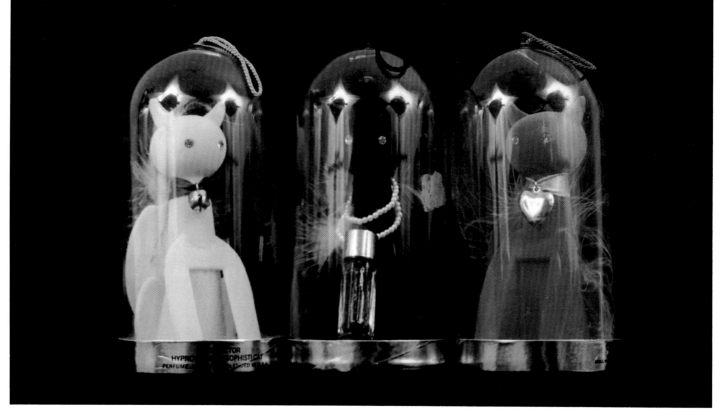

Meow!

A catty, colorful threesome...
Hypnotique Sophisti-Cats; Max Factor; probably 1950s.

In the paws of a 4-1/2" plush, green-eyed cat, a 2" vial of Max Factor's *Primitif*.

Golden Woods "Sophistic-Cat"; Max Factor; 1951.

Galloping into the sunset and Spring-time, this 2-1/2" vial of *Apple Blossom* by Lander astride a 4-1/2" golden horse.

Rudolph the Red-Nosed Reindeer; Rubicon; 1940s.

A collector's delight! Elvis Presley's *Teddy Bear*; 3" bottle; trademarked 1957.

Charming presentation of two die; bottles marked "guaranteed imported French perfume".

Just resting!

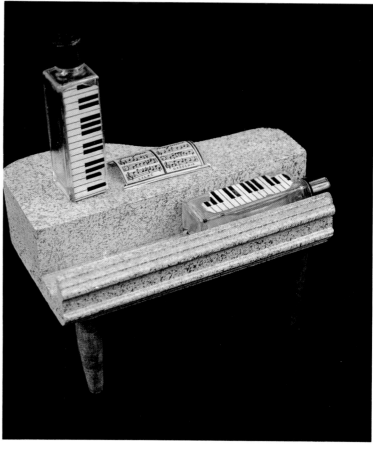

"Tickle the ivories"...the "piano" holds two "keyboard" bottles.

Two Dali-esque figures in a surrealistic setting.

"Steppin' out with my baby!" Gold shoes hold frosted vials, marked "Paris."

Each of these scenic topped boxes holds
10 miniatures.

Gardenia Cologne, Powder, and
Bubble Bath; Lander.

Petite Sauvage; 2-1/2"; Long Beach, California, Cosmetco; 1950s.

Bermuda Blue; 2-1/4" (bottle made in France), bluebird etched on stopper; Perfumeries Distributors, Hamilton, Bermuda; 1952.

Advertisement for *Escape* by Mary Dunhill, 1950s.

Beckon Essence; 1-1/2"; Fuller Brush Co., Hartford, Conn.

Chant D'Aromes; Guerlain.

Jili Parfum; 3", Perfumes by Wire,
Beverly Hills, Calif.

Arlene Richards, 3-1/2", Hamden,
Conn.

Debutante Mystic Moment Toilet Water; 1-3/4"; Fuller Brush Co., Distributed by Daggett & Ramsdell, Inc.

Carnegie Pink; Hattie Carnegie; 4-1/2" and 2-1/2" cologne and bath oil in boxed set with Carnegie's signature pink paper and ribbon.

Waves of Fragrance, Bourjois; 6-1/2" bottle.

Sables and Pearls; Saravel; pearlized
lift top box; modernistic bottle with the
look of a glistening ice cube.

Indiscrete;   3-3/4"; acrylic bow top.

A giant-sized beautician's special of
Revlon's *Intimate*, introduced in 1957.

Marked Schiaparelli, probably from the 1950s, this bottle contained an unknown fragrance.

Advertisement for *Yu*; Harriet Hubbard Ayer, 1950s.

Electrique; Max Factor; 3" x 1-1/4" blue "lightning bolt" presentation; 1954.

Ose; John Robert Powers (founder of the famed Powers Modeling Agency); 3-3/4"; French; initialed stopper; 1959.

Cabochard; Gres; 3-3/4" bottle marked Baccarat, made in France; 1958.

Midnight, Contraband, and *Bright Secret*, a Tussy Fragrance Trio in 4" three-sectioned folding box; each bottle 3" x 2", 1950s.

We Moderns cologne; Saks Fifth Avenue; 1959.

Arpege and *My Sin*; Lanvin.

Advertisement in 1955 issue of *L'Illustration* for *LaFraicheur Eau de Lanvin* .

My Sin; Lanvin; lipstick style case in 3-3/4" velour box, marked "Designed by Cartier. " Although this presentation was most likely from the 1950s, *My Sin* was introduced in 1923.

Toujours Moi; Corday; 2-1/4"; delicate ivory and gold top; 1951.

A dazzling array of Nina Ricci *L'Air du Temps* atomizers.

L'Heure Bleu; Guerlain. Although bottle is of early style, this presentation (in black leather travel sheath) was offered by Guerlain in the 1950s.

Detchema; Revillon; 3-1/2" bottle fits inside a black suede pouch that rests inside a 4" velour container; 1953.

Too hot to handle... *Flambeau*; Faberge; 3-3/8" bottle with gold-rimmed stopper sits on red velvet cushion in a white embossed case; 1955.

Spanning the decades, a triple threat from Lancome: *Bocages*, 1935; *Magi*, 1949; and *Tresor*, 1953.

Lasso; Patou; 2"; 1955.

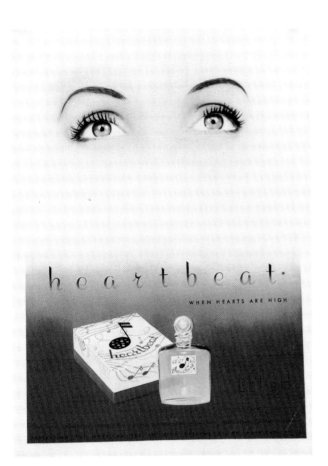

All in a row, *Cabochard* Gres factices in varying sizes, tallest 6-1/2"; 1959.

1950's advertisements for *Heartbeat* by Leigh.

Cabochard; by Gres; 3-3/4" bottle marked Baccarat; made in France; 1953.

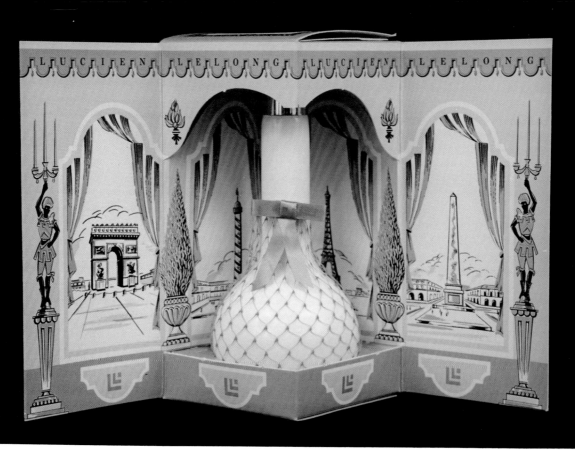

Lucien Lelong milk glass bottle in fold out display box.

Chouda; Gres; 1-1/2"; 1959.

Although introduced in 1932, this advertisment for *Vol de Nuit* by Guerlain appeared in 1957.

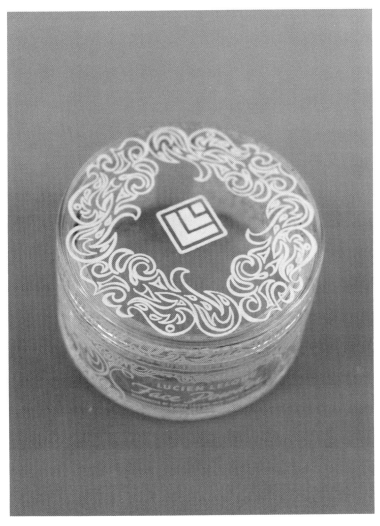

Decorative lucite container held Lucien Lelong Face Powder.

This urn-shaped bottle is marked Christian Dior.

A Christian Dior boxed trio: *Diorama*, 1947; *Miss Dior*, 1948; and *Diorissimo*, 1956.

With a Victorian look, *Night Blooming Cereus;* Scaglia; 1954.

Joya; Myrugia; 1954.

Hypnotique; Max Factor; 1-1/4" diameter, hinged bird's nest contains solid perfume.

Alma de Espana; Covescas Corp., N.Y.; 4".

Y; Yves Saint Laurent; 2-1/4" etched bottle in 3-1/4" lift-top box; 1964.

L'Interdit; Givenchy; 3-1/4"; 1957.

1000; Patou; Paris; 1950s.

L'Interdit; Givenchy; marbleized base
and top, acrylic lid.

Snob; LeGalion; 1952.

Les Yeux Doux; Forvil, Paris; 1950s.

With this card game sweeping the nation, what better name to usher in the Fifties than *Canasta* by Jacques Fath; 1950.

Coup de Feu; Marquay; 1957.

Plush, gold-tipped drawstring pouches hold an array of Marquay, Paris fragrances.

"Nestled all snug in their box," a Corday trio: *Le Gardenia*, *Le Muguet* and *Le Narcisse*; 1950s.

Ceil Bleue by famed couturier Ceil Chapman; 1950s.

Le Muguet Du Bonheur (1952), *Poivre* (1954) and the enduring *Le Narcisse Noir* (1912); Caron, Paris.

Dachelle; Lily Dache; 1962.

By the famed Hollywood couturier,
his own fragrance *Don Loper*; 8-1/4".
Photograph by Robert Ball.

The gold rush....*20 Carats* by Dana;
introduced in 1933.

What better landmark than the Eiffel
Tower brimming with perfume and
wrapped in cellophane!

Ecusson 88; Jean D'Albret.

Crystal "accordian-pleated" bottle; unknown scent and maker.

Secret de Suzanne; Maxim; 4".

Fete; Molyneux; 1962. Note: There was also a *Fete de Molyneux* in 1927.

Judith; 3", Judith Muller, Israel; probably 1960s.

Caleche; 4-3/4", Hermes; 1960s.

The flower garden...on left, *Oscar de la Renta*; on right, *Chloe*.

Infini; Caron; 1970.

Ghazi perfume by Barone, teams with Barone "firecracker" lipstick holder; 1972.

Designed in the 1970s by Elsa Paretti for her friend the couturier Halston, nee Roy Frowick, clean and beautiful shapes to hold soap, talcum powder, and perfume, along with a special Halston compact.

Anais Anais; Cacharel; 1-1/2"; 1978.
Bottle design by Annegret Beier.

For the neck or waist, a tasseled beauty!
1-5/8" bottle in a maroon flip-top container was used as a promotion for the introduction of Yves Saint Laurent's *Opium*; 1977.

Cachet; Prince Matchabelli; 1970.

Farouche; Nina Ricci; 2-1/4"; 1974.

Photographs courtesy of Parfums
Givenchy.

Cavale; Faberge; unusual hinged metal container with a turn-of-the-century look, case engraved with inset slots marked GBF Cavalle; 1975.

Parure; Guerlain; 3-3/4"; 1975.

The exotic *Opium*, introduced by Yves Saint Laurent in 1977.

Hermes Eau d' Cologne; 6-1/2"; introduced in 1979, the same year the Parfum Hermes factory was opened in Normandy.

Ylang, Ylang, 5" x 2-3/4" (bottle made
in France).

Must de Cartier;   2", Cartier, Paris,
1981.

A luminescent duo...*Luminere*;
Rochas; 6-1/4" and 5-1/4"; 1984.
Photograph by Robert Ball.

R.L.; 1-1/2"; Ralph Lauren.

Armani; 1-3/4"; Georgio Armani.

Norell; 3".

Quorum; 2-1/8"; Piug.

Lauren; 1-3/4"; Ralph Lauren.

Sophia; 2-1/2".

Pheromone; 2-1/2".

Lou Lou; 3-1/2"; CA Charel.

Red; 2-3/4"; Giorgio, Beverly Hills.

Paloma Picasso; 2-1/4" and 4"; 1984.

Sleek, obalesque design in purse size *Paloma Picasso* with its own velvet, drawstring bag.

Poison; 1-1/2", Christian Dior, 1986.

Poison Perfumed Talc.

Tiffany; 4-1/2"; Tiffany & Co.

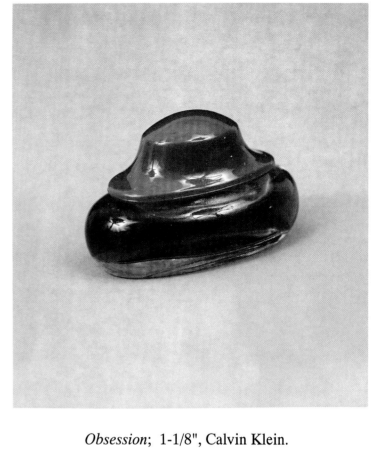

Obsession; 1-1/8", Calvin Klein.

Panthere de Cartier; 4-1/4"; 1987.

Caroline Amato; 3-1/2" bottle; made
in France; marked "C.023."

Nina; Nina Ricci; 5" x 3-1/2" frosted bottle marked Lalique, France; 1987.

Blazer; Anne Klein; Leo the lion label, in honor of Anne Klein's astrological sign; (discontinued).

Molinard de Molinard; 1982; Lalique.

Private Collection; Estee Lauder.

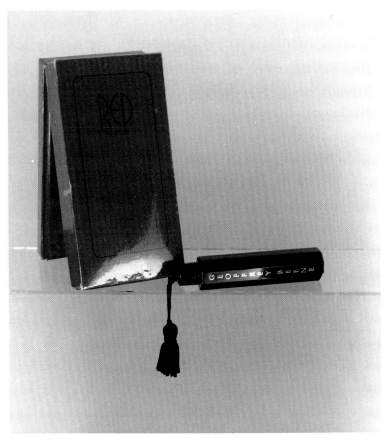

Red; Geoffrey Beane; 3"; discontinued; (not to be confused with Fred Hayman's *Red*.)

King Kong; de Kenzo; 5-1/2" x 2-1/2"; discontinued.

Already a classic, *Oscar de la Renta* perfume, powder jar, and frosted boudoir case.

"Old World" charm meets the needs of today's modern woman. From Austria, a hand-crafted needlepoint atomizer.

F'Sens; Sonia Rykiel; (discontinued).

Jontue Limited Edition; 4" x 4"; acid marked 480/1500-1982.

Niki De Saint Phalle by the sculptor herself; Paris, 1982; 4-3/4"; cobalt bottle with enameled plastic snakes on gold cover.

Updated and elegant...Guerlain's *Shalimar* encased in a 6-1/4" gold-latticed atomizer; dated 1981.

Fashion designer Romeo Gigli's cologne in award-winning bottle; early 1990s.

273 by Fred Hayman, Beverly Hills.

Montana; Claude Montana.

With a glittering bow top . . . *White Diamonds* by Elizabeth Taylor.

Sung, Alfred Sung; 5" x 3", current.

Charming *L'Air du Temps* by Ricci; 5-bottle miniatures in "springtime-inspired" presentation case; a recent "limited edition" offering.

Hubert de Givenchy poses beside a giant *Ysatis* factice to honor its introduction into the family of fine Givenchy fragrances. Photograph courtesy of Parfums Givenchy.

Factices

In rear, two giant sizes of Guerlain's *Chamade* (1969); largest is 9-1/2" x 6-1/4"; same bottle for *L'Heure Bleue* appears in front.

Casaque Parfumee 90; Jean d'Albret;
9" x 3-1/2"; 1950s.

Jolie Madame; Balmain; 11-3/4"; 1953.
Photograph by Robert Ball.

Caline; Patou; 8-1/2" x 7-1/2"; 1964.

Oscar de la Renta; 12"; 1977.

Poison; Christian Dior; 12" high, 9" wide.

Dune; Christian Dior; 10-1/2"; 1992.
Photograph by Robert Ball.

Mila Schoen Eaude Parfum; 10-1/2";
current. Photograph by Robert Ball.

Photograph courtesy of Regine de
Robien and Druout Galleries.

Section Three -
The Art of Collecting:
From Paris and New York

Recognizing the beauty of not only the fragrance but the manner in which it was presented, Regine De Robien is a pioneer in the appreciation of commercial fragrance bottles from the past, and has been instrumental in elevating them to collectible status throughout the world.

Following is an interview recorded in May 1993, which Regine de Robien has kindly agreed to share.

Q. *Regine, could you tell us how your love affair with perfume bottles began?*

A. First of all, I must tell you that I was an interior (architectural) decorator when the idea came to me, in 1980, to establish a gallery that featured perfume and beauty products. First I had to find a name, and finally decided on *Beaute Divine–Divine Beauty*. Caron Perfumes had used this name at the turn of the century, but they very kindly allowed me to use it when I opened my gallery.

Decorating the shop was a challenge. I decided to cover the walls with parfum and beauty advertisements and to place bottles of brand-name parfums on the furniture in my salon. Of course, this was especially effective on vanities and dressing tables. Most of these bottles were from the later years of the 19th century and the early 20th century. I chose them because of their colorful labels, their shapes, and purity of form. A collector by nature, my instinct told me that a pure example had to contain the original label and, if possible, the original box. In short order, people were bringing me their own bottles, which at the time held little appeal for them, to add to my decorating collection.

By 1982, I had progressed to placing these bottles in my windows and they attracted a somewhat different clientele than I had expected, consisting mainly of people who were in the perfume business themselves. In 1982, the time was not yet right. However, in my gallery on the Rue du Maroc, only the Lancome perfume called *Le Marrakech*, in its rare and sumptious box, attracted a collectible-minded person. This was Yves Saint Laurent, the recent proprietor of the Villa Majorelle in Marrakech.

George Vindry, founder of the International Museum of the Perfume of Grasse, encouraged me to move my gallery to the Rue Saint Sulpice, and also urged me to continue amassing my unique and rare treasures.

In the years 1980 to 1983, the Count Bruno d'Harcourt, a young collector who was only interested in parfums that told a story, discovered my collection, and was especially attracted to perfumes like the rare *Chateau d'Azur*, which was in the shape of a castle, the amusing *Roulette aux Parfum* by de Legrain, the rare and marvelous flacon for *Coueur en folie*, and the "Rosine" perfumes of Paul Poiret.

In 1984, Bruno d'Harcourt decided to sell his collection, the first public perfume catalog auction ever, which was held at the Hotel Drouot in Paris, and

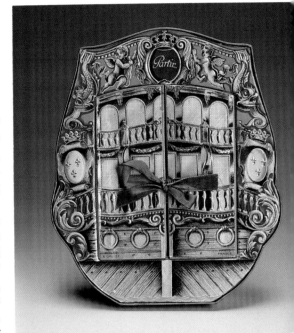

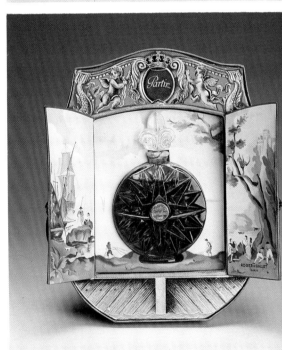

Partir by Roger et Gallet. Photographs courtesy of Regine de Robien and Druout Galleries.

Fontanis-Fontanis; Parfums de Rosine; "1925." Photograph courtesy of Regine de Robien and Drouot Galleries.

Grace; D'Orsay. Photograph courtesy of Regine de Robien and Drouot Galleries.

repeated in 1985 and 1986. I immediately alerted some of my dedicated collectors, including one couple from the United States, who passionately pursued exceptional pieces, always faithful to the cause. Since 1985 they have remained my friends.

Q. *But, Regine, how did you become an expert?*
A. After the first auction of Bruno d'Harcourt's collection, the commissioner at the gallery, Maitre Olivier Coutau-Begarie, asked me to do a catalog for the second sale, which they were planning to announce, featuring another collection of perfume bottles, for the success of the first auction had brought an influx of more wonderful bottles. Each year since 1986 we have organized an auction at the Paris Hotel Drouot, a big auction gallery from which prestigious perfume bottles continue to be sold.

Q. *Can you describe why these sales are so successful?*
A. They have attracted a huge clientele that come from all corners of France, as well as England, Switzerland, Belgium, Germany, in fact all of Europe–and especially those who cross the Atlantic from the United States. Many Japanese attend also. Some attend personally, and others send their representatives. The telephone lines are jammed. And, of course, the Hotel Drouot relies on its reputation as a fine auction house.

Q. *Regine, where do all these beautiful bottles come from?*
A. The reputation of the gallery speaks for itself, and in our last auction we counted no less than 68 consignees or sellers who brought us these bottles. The auctions have provided a tremendous boost to the perfume collector's industry. The catalogs, with their wonderful illustrations, are sold all over the world.

Q. *Can you share with us some interesting anecdotes you've encountered?*
A. One day a young woman came in to Beaute Divine and from her handbag she took out a dozen or so bottles–unopened and all containing the most wonderful and the best of Schiaparelli. She told me that each of the bottles had been given to her mother by her father, a great traveler, and also a womanizer, who used these perfumes as peace offerings when he wanted to be forgiven for his numerous pecadillos. I must keep his identity secret because this gentleman was well known around the world, especially by the press. That was why her mother never had the heart to open these bottles and they remained exactly as he had given them to her.

One evening a lady and her mother came to pay me a visit. The mother was in her seventies, and arrived holding a small package. The daughter instructed her to put it on the table. I was intrigued. Immediately the mother uncovered it, and inside was a small flacon box that had never been opened. Like a little girl, she proceeded to take off the ribbons so she could open the box and show me what was inside. First I saw a pure silk yellow material and then the beautiful perfume *Flausa* by René Lalique for Roger & Gallet. Everything was intact. For her, this perfume represented her mother. Her mother had this flacon on her dressing table and she wanted to open the perfume so that she could remember her again. However, I discouraged her and instead offered her 185,000 FF.

On another occasion the door of the Rue Saint-Sulpice opened and in came a poorly-dressed elderly gentleman, carrying an old perfume box, which he proceeded to talk to me about, for it contained certain bottles that he might want to sell. One by one I took them out, telling him that they were sumptious and much sought after and that I would buy them, knowing that collectors would gain knowledge by learning about them. One was *It's You* by Elizabeth Arden in its original box by Dufy, and representing, without doubt, the celebrated Diane Prize at the Exhibition at Chantilly. Among others, there were also Nina Ricci parfums in their mousseline plisse bags of rose, green and yellow. Thankfully, they had not lost any of their contents.

During a period of three years, this gentleman and I met on the last steps of the entrance to Beaute Divine, where the treasures he handled me never ceased to astound. I never met his friend but only saw her handwriting. Eventually the day came when this old lady mourned selling her last bottle. It was that which she treasured most...Coty's *L'Ambre Antique* by Rene Lalique. The perfume and it's rare coffret, double-wrapped in silk and also encased in sealed cellophane, had been made by Lalique for his friend Rene Coty.

At a flea market in Paris in 1985, an antique dealer of my acquaintance beckoned me over to show me her latest discovery. Lo and behold, she handed me a blue box. I opened it and inside was a bracelet with big imitation blue sapphires, separated by rhinestones. I said to her, "Linda, you know I don't sell costume jewelry," and she replied, "No, look closer! Look under the silk on the inside of the cover." When I did this I found an inscription that read *Le Parfum de Marcy*. With trembling hands, I lifted the piece upon which the bracelet rested and underneath were five little triangular flacons, which had never been opened, each with their original corks and labels, and each in the shape of a sapphire . . . part of this bracelet! What a marvelous discovery. I sold it to the Count d'Harcourt, who in turn put it in his auction sale, and this unique bracelet/flacon is now part of a beautiful collection belonging to someone in the United States.

Q. *Do you have any advice for collectors?*
A. Yes! First follow your instincts. They will be good. Then get to know your subject. There are three criteria: rarity, quality and the love of the item. The last is as important as the other two.

Q. *And finally, Regine, can you tell us which bottle is your favorite?*
A. I would have great difficulty trying to choose one before the other, knowing that the bottle I've never seen before always gives me goose bumps. However, *Le Roi du Soleil* always impressed me, and it's one of my favorites. But my heart and my taste always return to the marvelous bottles that Paul Poiret created for his perfumes de Rosine. The creativity, form, and originality of the materials he used warrants my admiration.

I know, however, that there is still much to be discovered, and it's this pursuit of the perfect bottle that remains to be found–in its perfect case–that will always excite me and give me the most pleasure. The bottle I haven't yet seen . . . that's my favorite bottle!

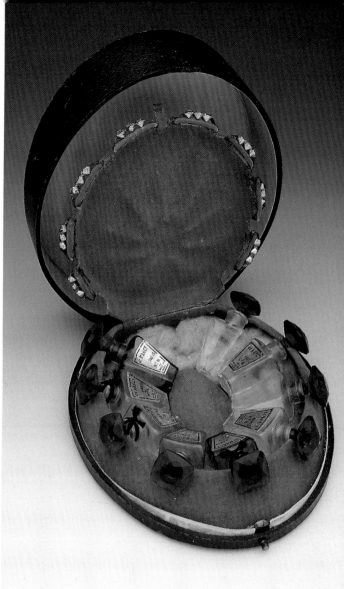

Collier; Les Parfums de Marcy. Photographs courtesy of Regine de Robien and Druout Galleries.

Tango; Gabilla. Photograph courtesy of Regine de Robien and Drouot Galleries.

Photograph courtesy of Regine de
Robien and Drouot Galleries.

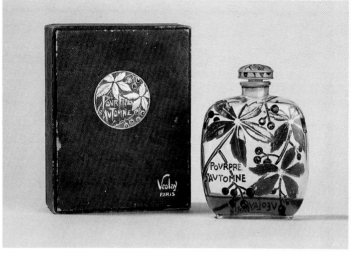

Bourpre d'Automne; Violet-Veolay. Photograph courtesy of Regine de Robien and Drouot Galleries.

Bal a'Versailles; Jean Desprez. Photograph courtesy of Regine de Robien and Drouot Galleries.

Gao; "Vallee des Roi;" L.T. Piver. Photograph courtesy of Regine de Robien and Drouot Galleries.

Ming Toy; Forest. Photograph courtesy of Regine de Robien and Drouot Galleries.

A Private Selection

On the following pages are a special assortment of commercial bottles from Ken Leach and Richard Peters, the proprietors of Gallery 57 in New York City. They will pique the interest of not only the seasoned collector but also anyone who appreciates the thrill of discovering the unusual, beautiful, and "not as frequently seen" examples of the bottle-makers' art.

Here too are many splendid presentations, each of which admirably reinforces the importance of not only the bottles but the ambiance of the complete product...from coffrets and colors to the aura of mystery and sumptious luxury that surrounds them. Although these examples are perhaps more difficult to find or more costly than most, seeing them displayed here will, hopefully, widen the search...and cause any dedicated aficionado's heart to beat just a little bit faster!

Parfum B; Lucien Lelong, Paris; early 1930s; 2"; painted metal bust lifts to reveal a tester-form bottle with dauber.

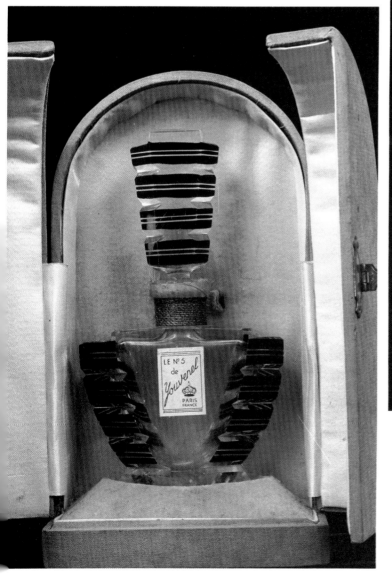

Le No. 5 de Youvenel; Youvenel, Paris; early 1930s; 5-1/4", enameled French crystal.

Ming; Babani, Paris; 1920; 4-1/2";
etched and enameled crystal.

Ingenious! *Clips-Parfum Jabot*;
Lucien Lelong, Paris; 1939; 2-1/4";
spring back mechanism allows bottles
to be worn as elegant dress clips.

Faoen; Park and Tilford; 4-1/2"; 1926.

Poudre De Rosine, Nuit De Chine powder box; Paul Poiret.

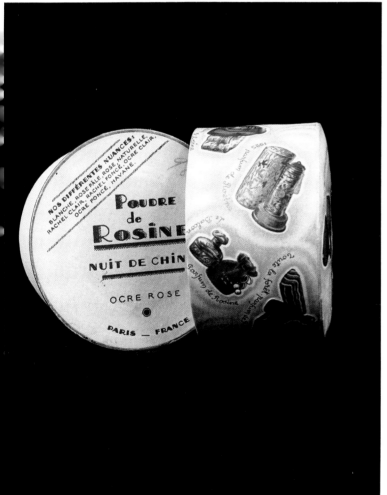

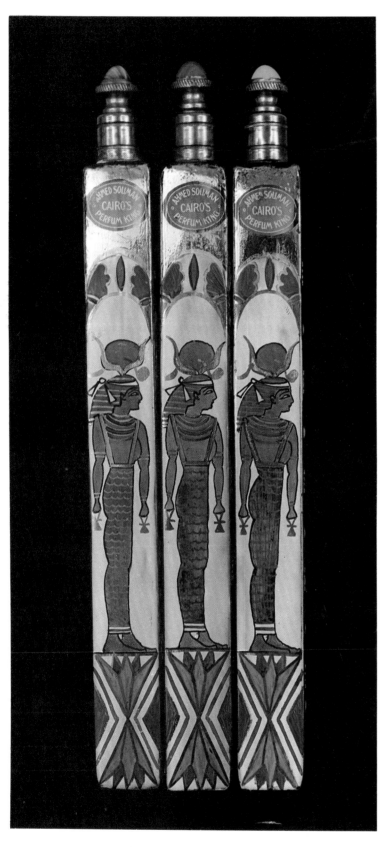

Sphinx; Dralle, Hamburg; late 1920s; 4-1/2"; crystal bottle and stopper with hinged metal cover.

Sandalwood, Rose, and *Lotus Flower*; Ahmed Soliman, Cairo; 1920s; 7-1/2"; Czech glass with enamel and gilt decoration, metal screw tops.

Antique Amber; Ahmed Soliman; Cairo; 3"; 1920s; Czech crystal bottle, interior and exterior painted metal, screw top with faux jewel.

Un Peu De Bonheur; Elizabeth Arden,
N. Y.; 3-1/4"; 1920s; label on bottom.

Parfum Pour Brunes; Lionceau, Paris;
4"; 1927

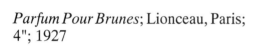

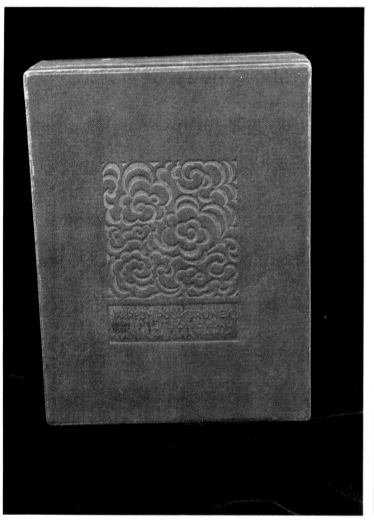

Pagoda; Ravel, N. Y.; 1945; 3-1/2";
gilt trim bottle with stopper of four
elephants.

Three Flowers Toilet Water; 6-1/2";
Richard Hudnut, N. Y. , Paris; 1920s.

Nuit De Chine; Rosine (Paul Poiret),
Paris; 7"; late 1920s.

Muguet; Harriet Hubbard Ayer, N. Y.;
3-1/2"; late 1920s.

Niradjah; Marquis, Paris; 1923;
3-3/4"; black glass bottle with painted
stopper.

From the mid-1920, a folding window
display for *Cheramy*, Paris; 21" high.

Advertising fan for Parfums Galeries
Lafayette *M'Lati* ,; signed Jack Rob-
erts, 1924.

With the Mailcoach; Mouson
Lavendar; 3"; Frankfort; 1950s.

Three Flowers gift set; Richard Hudnut,
N. Y.; mid 1920s.

Shocking; jewelled purse flacon; 2-1/2"; Schiapparelli, Paris; late 1940s.

Advertising fan for *Parfum Floramye*; L. T. Piver, Paris; 1923; signed G. Delaittre.

Drifting; Lilly Dache, Paris; 3"; late
1940s; Baccarat crystal.

Advertising fan for *Toute La Provence*;
Molinard Jeune, Paris; late 1920s;
signed U. Ganne.

Narceisse Bleu; Mury, Paris; 1925;
3"; blue wash on bottle, cobalt glass
stopper.

Hahna La Fleur Secrete; Rosine (Paul
Poiret), Paris; 3-3/8"; 1922.

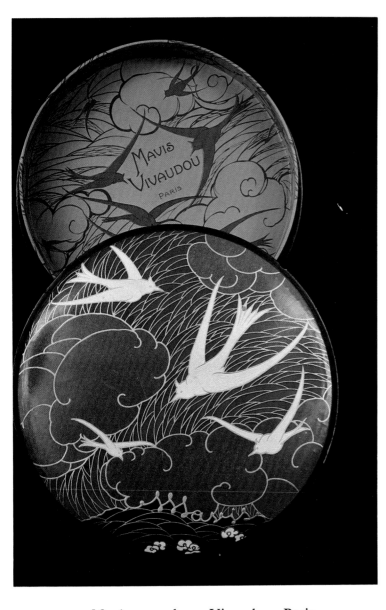

Mavis soap box; Vivaudou, Paris;
9-1/2" diameter; early 1920s.

Le Val Creux; Grasse, Paris; c. 1928.

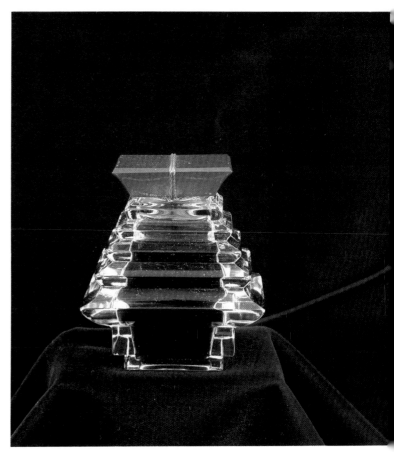

Bamboo; Weil, Paris; 1934; 3-1/2";
enameled glass stopper.

Paper fan for *Royal Origan* perfume,
Galeries Lafayette, Paris 1920s.

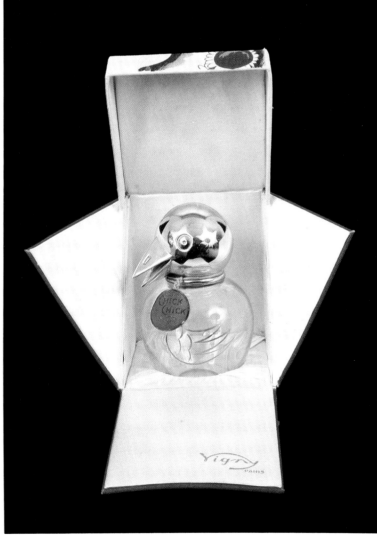

Le Chick Chick; Vigny, Paris; 1924; 5-
1/8"; metal stopper cover.

Roy Le Veuit; Marcel Guerlain, Paris; 1926; 3-1/8"; gilt trim.

Fille D'Eve Eau de Toilette; Nina Ricci; 1952; 8-3/4"; Lalique.

Jessamine O'Devon Toilet Water; Yardley, London; 1920; 4"; hand-finished, gilt crystal.

Tailspin; Lucien Lelong, Paris; 1962; 5"; glass and enameled metal.

Couer Joie; Nina Ricci, Paris; 1947; 4-1/4"; Lalique glass, graphics by Berard.

Unknown scent by Ota, Paris; 3"; early 1930s.

Duska; Langlois (United Drug Co.),
Boston; 1920s; 4-1/4"; face powder,
rouge, perfume and toilet water.

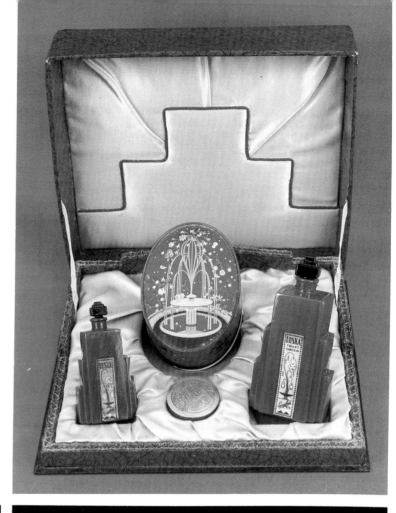

Stradivari soap; Prince Matchabelli,
N. Y.; 1950s.

Chouki; Coryse, Paris; late 1920s;
4-1/8"; Baccarat with gilt trim.

Sortilege Stork Club; Paris; late 1940s;
7-1/2"; carved wooden bird, cork-fit-
ted stopper; identical to table vases at
New York's "society mecca," the Stork
Club.

Hallo Coco; Jovoy, Paris; 1924;
enameled glass stopper.

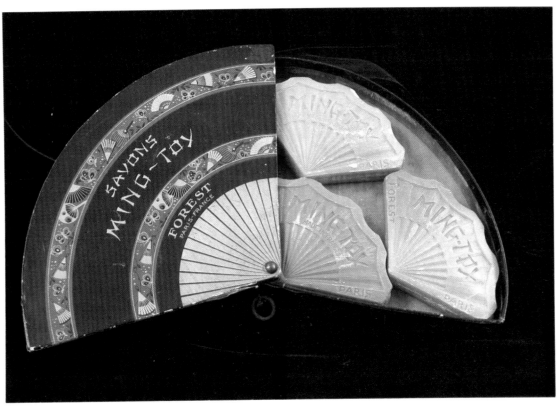

Ming Toy soap; Forest, Paris; 1924.

Dark Brilliance; Lentheric; Chicago; 3"; Paris, New York; 1946.

Tresor; Lancome, Paris; 1952; 4"; crystal bottle with metal screw cap; design by Georges Delhomme.

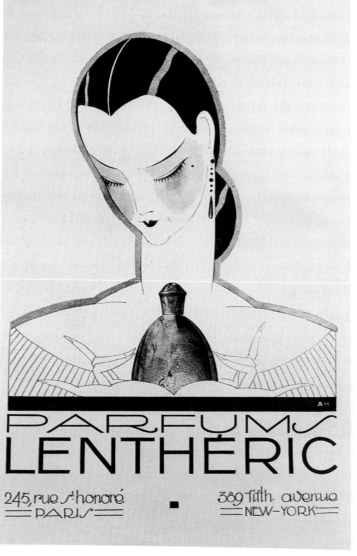

An Art Deco ad for Lentheric perfumes featuring a *Miracle* bottle, mid 1920s.

Flamme De Glorie; Pleville, Paris;
Bacarrat; 3-1/2"; 1924.

Violet Simplicity; 6-1/4"; late teens.

Feerie; Rigaud, Paris; 1940; box illustration by J. G. Domergue is under
glass.

Asso Di Cuori (Ace of Hearts); 3";
Bertelli, Milan; late 1930s; metal screw
tops.

No. 450; Elizabeth Arden; 3"; 1940s.
(Ms. Arden's opera box number was
450!)

Contessa Azzura, GI. VI. Emme, Milan,
2-1/2" 1922.

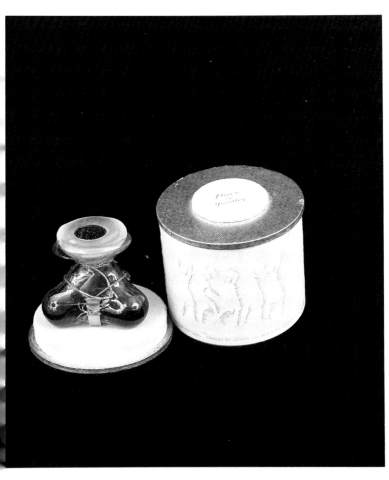

Flair; Yardley, London; 1-5/8"; 1952.

Caranomi; Langlois, Boston; 4-1/2";
1920; Baccarat.

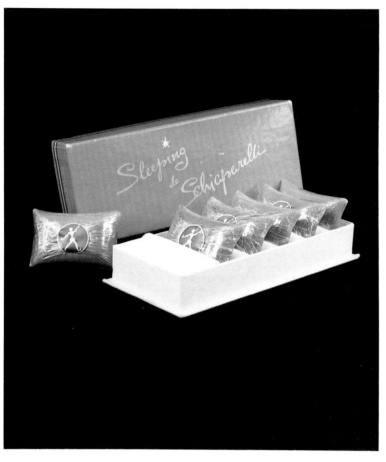

Sleeping soaps; Schiaparelli, Paris; 1938.

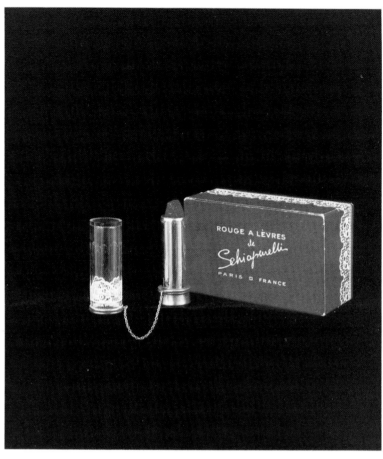

Shocking lipstick; Schiaparelli, Paris; mid-1940s; glass cover.

Party Package; Schiaparelli, Paris; 1940s; favors hold 3" cylindrical bottles of *Succes Fou*, *Sleeping* and *Shocking*

Shocking; Schiaparelli, Paris; 1940s.

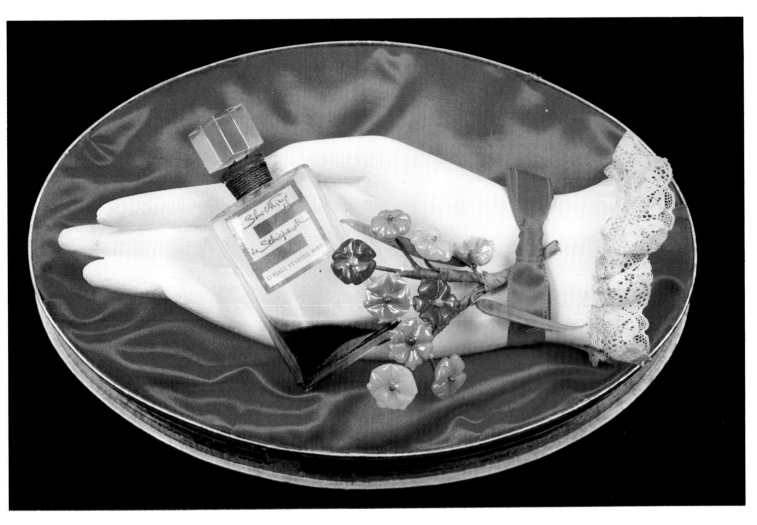

Shocking; Schiaparelli, Paris; 1940s;
3-1/4"; composition hand holds square
form bottle, glass flowers.

Shocking soaps; Schiaparelli, Paris; late
1940s.

Shocking soaps; Schiaparelli, Paris;
1938.

It's You in miniature pinch bottle; Elizabeth Arden, N. Y.; 1940s.

Gala; El Morocco Perfumes, N. Y.; late 1940s; 4-1/2";French bottle, box design by Jave Fabry.

The Golden Arrow; John Frederics, N.Y.; 1935; 3"; gilt glass dauber stopper.

Unknown scent by Marquis, Paris; 4";
mid-1920s.

Belle De Jour; D'Orsay, Paris &
N.Y.; lucite stopper; 1940.

Vocalise; Rimmel, Paris; 1923; 4";
Baccarat, metal stopper cover.

Bouquet Belle De Jour; D'Orsay, Paris;
5-1/4"; created to celebrate the 25th
anniversary of D'Orsay in America;
1940; lucite stopper, cork fit.

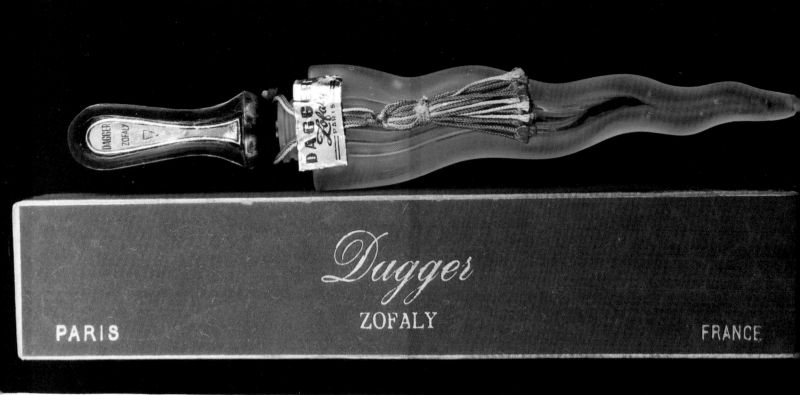

Dagger; Zofaly, Paris; 8-1/2" curva-
ceous flacon of frosted glass with black
glass stopper; 1940s.

Love Potion; Charles of the Ritz, New
York; 1942; 6-1/2"; gilt glass stopper
with cork fitting.

Magie and *Tresor*; Lancome, Paris;
1952; 3-1/4"; designed by Georges
Delhomme; metal screw caps.

L'Heur; Volay of Paris; late 1940s.

Tresor; Lancome, Paris; 1959; 2-3/4";
opalescent glass, metal screw top; bottle
design by Georges Delhomme to sa-
lute the launch of the Russian space-
craft Sputnik.

Slumber Song; Helena Rubenstein,
N.Y., 1938; 6-1/2".

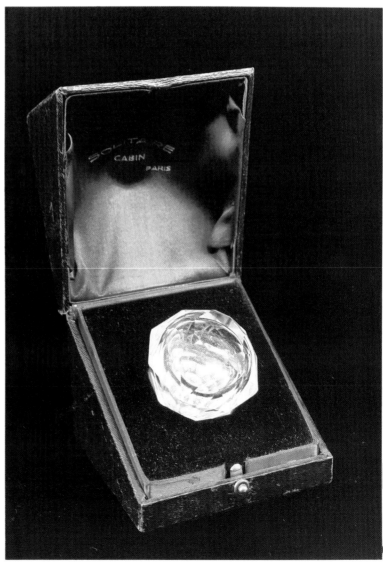

Miss Kate; Bourjois, Paris; 4-1/2";
early teens; black glass stopper.

Circe; Moiret, Paris; 1925; 3"; black
glass.

Solitaire; Cabin, Paris; 1930s; 1-3/4"
diameter; metal screw cap is hidden.

Vol De Nuit;   Guerlain, Paris; box design.

PARFÚMS LUCIEN LELONG

Lucien LeLong ad, early 1950s.

Quick Change;   Lucien Lelong; late 1940s; a 2" three-color lipstick coat clip.

Floral Jockettes; Karoff, N.Y.; 2-5/8";
1937; wooden screw tops.

Mah-Jongg; Pleville, Paris; 1924;
4-1/4"; a jade green stopper on a black
bottle with painted recessed design.

La Fete Des Roses; Caron, Paris; 1949;
4-1/8"; the gilded glass bottle rests in a
drawer of silk rose petals. As the drawer
is pulled from its cover, the petals fall
free.

Royal Bain De Champagne ad for Caron, mid-1940s.

Avant La Fete (4-3/4") and *Fete Mondaine* (8-3/4"); De Vibour, Paris; late 1930s; black glass with gilding.

No 1; La Cloche, Paris, 1940s; 3-3/4"; gilded glass.

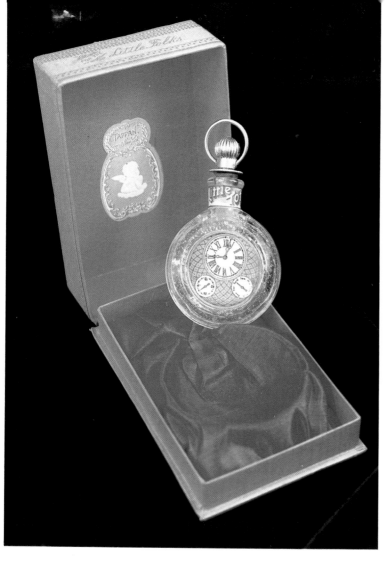

Ambre Indien; Volnay, Paris; 1928; 5-1/8"; black glass.

Little Tot; Tappan, NY.; early 1900s; 3-1/2"; metal and cork stopper.

Xmas Morn; company unknown; France; 5-1/2"; 1920s.

L'Amour Dans Le Coeur; Arys, Paris; 4-3/4"; 1919.

Ode; Guerlain, Paris; 1955; 6-1/2";
Baccarat.

This French Guerlain ad from 1959
offers a purse flacon with eleven fragrance choices.

Quand ?; Corday, Paris; 1930; 5"; gilt
black glass.

Sevres; Sauze Freres, Paris; 1939;
6-1/2"; cream and gold Sevres
porcelain bottle with cork plug.

Valencia; Marques De Elorza, Paris; 1929; aqua glass stopper.

Violette Fleur; Oriza L. Legrand; early 1920s; 4-1/2"; Baccarat.

Les Violettes; Molinard, France; 1917; 3-1/2"; Baccarat.

Gardenia; Renaud, Paris; mid-1920s; 6-1/8"; opaque white glass.

Ambre De Delhi; Babani, Paris; 1920;
5-1/4"; black and gold gilt decoration.

Les Seves; L'ary, Paris; 6"; late teens.

Ancien; Violet, Paris; 1922; 5" bottle
is finished and decorated to resemble
ancient glass.

Le Trefle Incarnat; L. T. Piver, Paris;
4-1/2"; 1890s.

Fragrance unknown; Myon, Paris; 1928; 2-3/8"; Baccarat, gold decoration on black glass, enameled metal cap over stopper.

Amour Sauvage; Ybry, Paris; 1925; 2-3/4; Baccarat, silver label and enameled silver cap over black glass stopper.

Byzance; Grenoville, Paris; 1930s; 4-1/4"; black glass, metal stopper cover.

Ah!! Paris; 4-3/4"; created for the City of Paris Department Store in San Francisco; 1924; Baccarat.

Le Lilas; H. Muraour, France; 4-1/4"; early 1920s; Baccarat.

Dashing; Lilly Dache, Paris; 3".

Drifting; Lilly Dache, Paris; 1942; 3-1/4"; a miniature made of composition with a glass stopper.

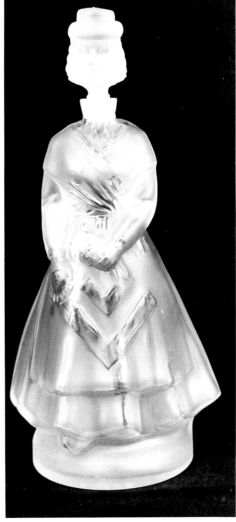

Scent unknown; Pages, France; 8-3/4".

Sleeping; Schiaparelli, Paris; 3-3/4"; mid-1940s; a leather purse case offering the choice of four scents.

Sweet Bye and Bye; Tappan, N. Y.; 1881; 2" glass bottle in metal holder.

225

Le Soir Ou Jamais; Chez Pompadour, Offenthal, Paris; mid-1920s; 3-1/2".

Merry Christmas; Benoit, Paris; 1928; 4-1/2"; black glass with gold decoration.

Oriental; Robert, N. Y.; mid-1920s; 3-3/4"; glass with painted finish.

Lillian Russell; Lillian Russel, N.Y.; late 1890s.

Fleurisette; Rowsky, Paris; 1920s;
enameled glass.

Vivante; Lournay, Paris; 1923; 6-1/4".

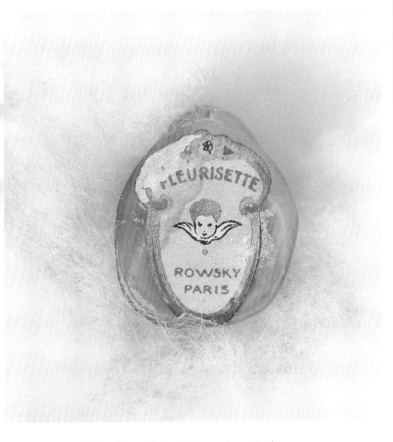

Fleurisette label; Rowsky, Paris.

Faisa; Myrugia Barcelona; 3-1/4";
early 1930s; black glass bottle with
white glass stopper rests in a brass cup
on a wooden base.

1949 ad for six Lanvin scents.

LANVIN PARFUMS

68

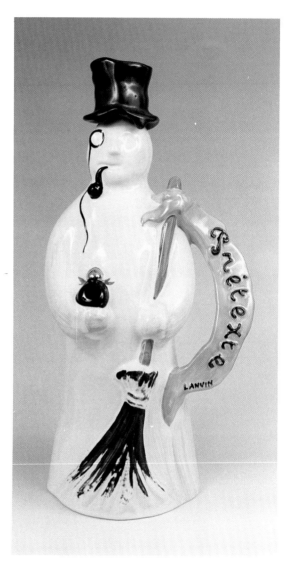

Lanvin counter display bottles designed by Yves Lanvin in 1950; 9-1/8"; French porcelain with paper labels.

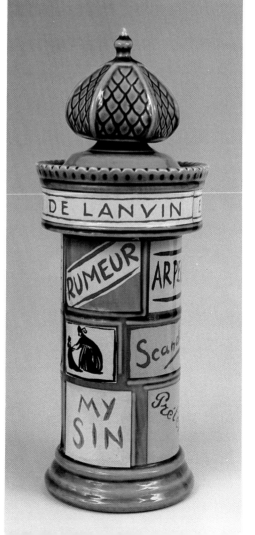

Muguet Fleuri; Oriza L. Legrand, Paris; 1920; 4-5/8" Baccarat bottle with enameled decoration.

Monjoly; Lubin, Paris; mid-1920s; 4"; black enameling and gilt stopper.

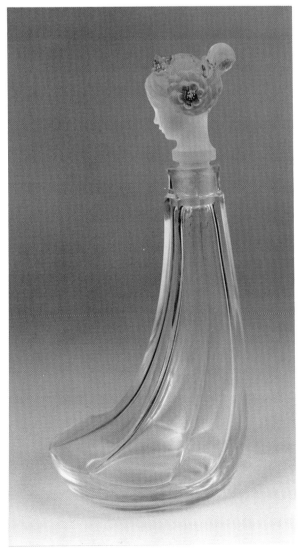

A 1925 illustration by Pesle for *Amaryllis* by Lubin of Paris.

Magda; Lubin, Paris; 1923; 5-1/8"; Baccarat.

Sphinx D'or; Ramses, Paris; 1923; 3";
Sphinx conceals glass stopper.

Enigma; Lubin, Paris; 1925; 3-1/2";
gilt crystal.

Early 1920's ad for the French porcelain company Robj shows a selection
of perfume lamps and burners.

Tutankamen; Casa Nancy, Paris; mid
1920s; 4-3/4". This preparation was
intended for use in perfume lamps and
burners.

Scent unknown; France 1920s; 4-1/8".

Ramses, Sidon, Paris; 3-/14"; early 1920s.

Ambre De Nubie; Ramses, Paris; 1922.

Vallee Des Rois; L. T. Piver, Paris; 1925; 5-1/4"; enameled Baccarat crystal.

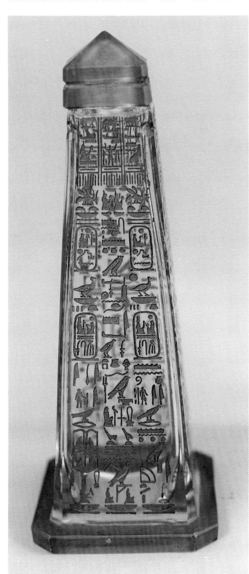

Ramses II; Bichara, Paris; 8-1/8"; early 1920s.

Hotel Meurice; Paris; mid-1920s;
2-1/4"; metal bottle with faux amber
on screw top.

Jasmin; Bernard et Roger, Paris;
3-1/4"; early 1920s.

L'Envoutement; A. Gravier, Paris;
4-3/4"; early 1920s; Baccarat, gilded
and enameled.

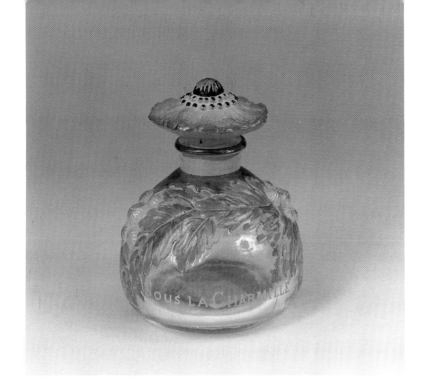

Sous La Charmille; P. Becher, Paris;
2-3/4"; late teens; enameled glass.

Le Lys Noir; Isabey, Paris; 1924;
5-1/2"; heavy black satin.

Le Jade; Roger et Gallet, Paris; product array includes a powder tin and
perfume box signed R. Lalique; 1923.

Fox Trot; Arys, Paris; 4-1/8"; black
stain; 1920.

La Plus Belle; Corday, Paris; 3-1/4";
Baccarat with gold decoration; 1927.

L'Heure Est Venue; De Marcy, Paris; 2-3/4"; metal and cork stopper; early 1900s.

Masque Rouge; Marcel Guerlain, Paris; 4" Eau De Toilette with face powder; 1927.

Cover de Femme; Myon, Paris; 3-1/4"; cased green Baccarat glass with enameled metal stopper cover and label; 1933.

An unknown scent from a French maker; 3-7/8"; 1920s.

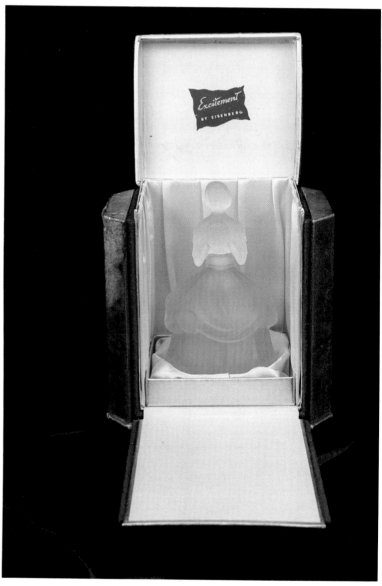

Eisenberg's *Excitement* line included *Stirring, Startling,* and *Enticing,* each in the original 1938 figural bottle.

Carnegie Blue; Hattie Carnegie, N.Y.; late 1940s; 3-1/4".

Golliwog cream pot; Vigny, Paris; 1924; 4-1/4"; frosted glass bottom with black and white glass cover.

Guili-Guili; Vigny, Paris; 1934; 6-1/4"; composition head covers glass stopper.

Sourire De France; Fontanis, Paris; 3-3/4"; 1926; pink opaque Baccarat glass with an enameled metal stopper cover.

Folie Bleue; Godet, Paris; 4-1/2"; mid 1920s.

Unknown French scent from the late teens; metal cover signed "M. Pautot;" 1-3/4".

Mon Yvonnet; Rimmel, Paris; 3-1/2"; early 1920s.

236

Xantho; Gabilla, Paris; 1927; 2-1/8";
Baccarat.

Memoire Cherie; an Easter presentation by Elizabeth Arden, N. Y.; 1959.

Gotic; Gueldy, Paris; 3-3/4"; 1922.

A 1960 Mary Chess catalogue page shows large glass chessmen bottles on a board; priced then at $100.

Spice Box; Mary Chess, N. Y.; 1962; tallest piece 3-1/8".

Pois De Senteur; Nissery, Paris; 3-5/8"; early 1920s.

Indian Summer; Esme of Paris; 1946;
3-1/4"; gilt and enameled glass with
dauber stopper.

Pense Moi; R. Louis, Paris; 1930;
2-3/4"; silver gilt on crystal, metal
screw stopper cover with gray stain.

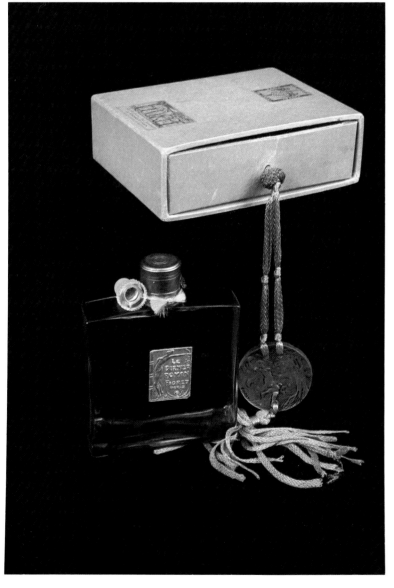

Le Dernier Roman; Fioret, Paris;
3-3/8"; 1925; hinged metal stopper
cover, glass pendant on box.

Bronze counter display for Fioret, Paris;
wood nymphs frolic among the twist-
ing trees; 3' x 3'.

Muguet; Guerlain, Paris; 3-3/4"; c. 1940; (reissue of a 1908 flacon).

Jicky; Guerlain, Paris; 1945; 4"; cobalt and crystal.

Gardenia; Molinelle, England; 2-3/4" square form; bottle resembling a box, separates to reveal a gilt stopper showing Cupid and Psyce blowing heart-shaped bubbles; 1935.

Parfum Maya; Lunya, Paris; 1923; 3-3/4"; painted stopper and decorative accents.

Saigon; Babani; Paris; 3-3/8"; opaque faux lapis glass with gilt trim; 1928

A May Morning; Esme of Paris; 4-1/4"; 1941.

Truso; D'Ciny, Paris; 2-3/4"; early 1920s.

Fleurs De Reine; Godet, Paris; early 1920s; 5-3/8"; Baccarat gilded crystal on a brass foot.

Coup De Fouet; Caron, Paris; 8"; gilt and enameled crystal; 1954.

Peter Pan opaline powder in silk jewel case; Fallis, Inc.; 1920s

Toute Le Foret; Rosine (Paul Poiret),
Paris; 1925.

Petit Mimosa; Caron, Paris; 1917.

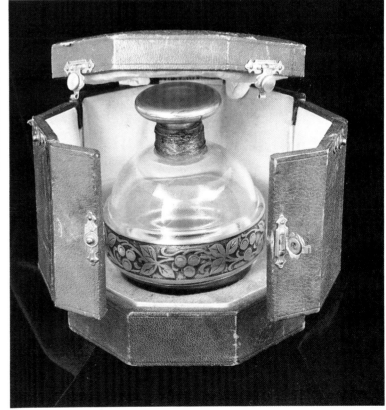

Unknown fragrance by Marquis, Paris;
3-1/2"; gilt art glass; early 1920s.

Byzance; Grenoville, Paris; 1926; 3-5/6"; Baccarat black glass bottle and cover.

Chypre; A. A. Vantines, N. Y.; 1930s; 3-1/8"; black glass

Fidelwood; The House of Fragrance, Bermuda; 3-1/4; crystal with black and gold decoration; 1937.

Unknown French scent from the late 1920s; 3-1/2".

A 1938 ad for Worth shows the R. Lalique sailboat bottle for *Projets* .

Esbroufe; Grenoville, Paris; 5-3/4"; 1940s; gilded blass.

1944 ad for Marny gift set.

Value Guide

These values represent a general assessment of current market conditions. Be aware that many factors influence variations in price, including the location and type of shop, condition of the bottle in question, and the trends of the fragrance bottle collecting world. These evaluations are meant to serve merely as guidelines; collectors must also rely on their own good judgement and common sense.

The first column indicates the page number on which a bottle can be found. The second column indicates the bottle's position on that page–**R**ight, **L**eft, **T**op, **B**ottom etc. The last column provides the value range, in U.S. dollars.

Page	Position	Value	Page	Position	Value	Page	Position	Value
7	R	under $100 each	38	TR	75-100	61	TL	under $100
8	T	under $100		BR	under $100		TR	30-60
	B	500-1000	39	L	75-100		BL	under $100
9	T	50-75 each		TR	100-200		BR	25-50
10	T	125-175	40	TL	under $100	62	TR	under $100
	B	75-100		TR	under $100 each		BR	75-100
11	B	under $100		BL	75-100	63	TL	25-50
12	T	under $100	41	C	75-100		TR	under $100
13	B	100-200	42	B	under $100 each		BL	75-100
19	T	75-100	43	TL	75-100	64	L	75-100
	B	under $100		TR	under $100		TR	75-100
20	T	75-100		BR	75-100		BR	under $100
	B	under $100	44	TL	20-40	65	TL	under $100 each
22	T	75-100		TR	150-200		TR	100-200
	B	100-150		BL	50-75		BL	200-300
	R	75-100	45	T	100-200		BR	75-125
23	TL	75-100		BL	30-60	66		75-100
	TR	75-100		BR	75-100	67	ALL	300-500
	BL	under $100	46	L	75-100	68	TL	300-500
	BR	75-100		TR	20-40		TR	75-100
24	T	75-100		BR	100-200		BL	under $100
	BL	50-75	47	T	100-150	69	TL	50-75
	BC	50-75		BL	75-100		TR	75-100
	BR	100-150		BC	75-100		BL	under $100
25	TL	under $100		BR	under $100		BR	75-100
	TC	under $100	48	TL	75-100	70	TR	50-75
	TR	75-100		R	75-100		BL	200-300
26	TL&R	150-250	49	ALL	under $100 each	71	L	25-50
27	TL	25-40	50	TL	100-200		TR	under $100
	TR	25-50		BL	under $100		BR	75-125
	BL	under $100		BR	under $100	72	TL	under $100
	BR	under $100	51	ALL	under $100 each		TC	25-50
28	TL	75-100	52	TL	75-100		TR	under $100
	TR	under $100		TR	75-100		B	under $100
	BL	under $100		BL	75-125	73	TR	under $100
	BR	75-100		BR	under $100		BL	under $100
29	TL	75-100	53	TL	75-100		BR	under $100
	BL	75-100		TR	under $100	74	TL	25-50
30	TL	75-100		BL	under $100 each		BL	under $100
	TR	under $100		BR	25-50		BR	75-100
	BL	100-150	54	TL	under $100	75	TL	under $100
	BR	100-150		TR	75-100		TR	40-60
31	TL	75-100	55	TL	under $100		BL	75-100
	TC	25-50		BL	75-100		BR	under $100
	TR	75-100	56	TL	25-50	76	TL	75-125
	BL	30-60		TR	50-75		TR	25-50
	BR	75-100		BL	75-100		C	under $100
32	ALL	under $100 each		BR	under $100		BL	75-100
33	TL	75-100	57	ALL	under $100 each		BR	75-100
	BL	under $100	58	TL	under $100	77	TL	under $100
34	TL	100-150		TR	100-200		TC	30-60
	TR	75-100		BL	under $100		TR	30-60
35	BL	75-100		BR	under $100		BL	50-75
	TR	50-100	59	TL	25-50		BR	under $100
36	TL	30-60		TR	75-100	78	TL	300-500
	TR	75-100		BL	under $100		B	500+
	BL	75-100		BR	100-200	79	TL	40-60
	BR	100-200	60	TL	under $100		TR	50-75
37	TL	50-100		TR	under $100		BL	25-45
	BL	75-100		BL	25-50		BR	under $100
	TR	50-75		BR	25-50			

Page	Position	Price
80	TL	35-50
	TR	50-75
	BL	under $100
	BR	75-100
81	TL	50-75
	TR	100-200
	BL	50-75
	BR	50-75
82	TL	75-100
	TR	100-150
	BL	100-150
	BR	under $100
83	T	75-100
	BL	under $100
	BR	75-100
84	L	50-75
	TR	under $100
	BR	75-100
85	TL	50-75
	TR	under $100
	BL	35-60
86	T	40-60
	BL	100-200
	BR	under $100 each
87	TL	50-75
	TR	20-30
	BL	under $100
	BR	30-50
88	T	100-150 (chess piece)
		25-50 (perfume holder)
		75-100 (*Je Reviens*)
	BL	30-50 each
	BR	75-100
89	TL	under $100
	TR	75-100
	BL	45-65
	BR	under $100
90	TL	75-100
	TR	75-100
	BL	75-100
	BR	under $100
91	TL	under $100
	TR	under $100
	BL	500+
	BR	75-100
92	L	30-50
	TR	75-125 each
	BR	50-75
93	TL	under $100
	TR	under $100
	BL	50-75
95		under $100
96	TL	under $100
	TR	75-100
	BL	under $100
97	TL	40-65
	BL	100-200
98	TL	75-100
	R	50-75
	BL	75-100
99	TR	50-75
	BL	under $100
100	TL	35-50
	TR	under $100
	BL	35-50 each
	BR	35-50
101	TL	50-75
	BR	100-200
102	T	75-150
	BL	under $100
	BR	under $100
103	ALL	under $100 each
104	TL	under $100
	BR	35-50
104	TL	under $100
	BR	35-50
105	TL	75-100
	BL	40-60
	BR	under $100
106	T	100-200
	B	100-200
107	TL	under $100
	TR	35-50
	BL	under $100
	BR	75-100
108	TL	under $100
	TR	under $100
	BL	under $100
109	TL	25-50
	TR	under $100
	BR	25-50
110	TL	50-75
	R	under $100
111	TL	75-100
	TR	75-100
	BL	500+, each
112	TL	under $100
	BR	under $100
113	BL	under $100
	BC	40-60
	BR	75-100
114	T	20-30
	B	under $100
115	BL	20-40
	R	150-200
116	TL	under $100
	TR	75-100
	B	75-100
117	TL	35-50
	TR	30-45
	BL	under $100
	BR	25-50
118	TL	75-100
	TR	100-150
	BL	200-250
	BR	75-100
122	ALL	under $100 each
123	T	500+, each
	BL	under $100
	BR	under $100
124	ALL	under $100 each
125	ALL	under $100 each
126	ALL	under $100 each
127	ALL	under $100 each
128	ALL	under $100 each
129	ALL	under $100 each
130	ALL	under $100 each
131	ALL	under $100 each
132	ALL	under $100 each
133	T	under $100
	BR	under $100
134	ALL	under $100 each box
135		50-75
136	TL	75-100
	TR	75-100
	BR	under $100
137	TL	under $100
	TR	75-100
	BR	under $100
138	TL	under $100
	R	75-125
	BL	40-60
139	T	75-100
	BL	75-100
	BR	25-50
140	TL	under $100
	BL	75-100
	BR	75-100
141	TL	75-100
	BL	under $100
	R	65-100
142	TL	35-50 each
	BL	50-65
143	T	50-65
	TL	35-50 each
	TR	75-100
	B	75-100
144	T	75-100
	BL	75-100 each
	BR	25-50
145	TR	35-75 each
	BR	75-100
146	T	75-100
	BL	40-65
147	TL	40-65
	TR	50-75
	B	200-300
148	TL	75-100
	TC	75-100
	TR	35-50
	BL	15-25
	BR	under $100
149	TL	under $100
	TR	75-100
	BL	50-75
	BR	75-100
150	TL	75-100
	TR	75-100
	CL	75-100
	B	100-200
151	T	75-100
	BL	75-100
	BR	75-100
152	TL	75-100
	TR	100-200
	BL	75-100
	BR	75-100
153	TL	75-100
	TR	under $100
	B	75-100
154	TL	75-100
	TR	75-100
	B	50-75
175		100-200 each
176	L	100-150
	R	150-250
177	L	150-200
178	L	200-300
	R	200-250
187	L	500-1000
	R	500-1000
188	TL	300-500
	B	300-500
189	T	500-1000
190	TR	500-1000
	BL	300-500
	BR	300-500
191	TR	1000+
	B	1000+
192	L	100-300
	TR	100-300
	BR	300-500
193	L	500-1000
	TR	500-1000
194	BL	100-300
	BR	100-300
195	T	500-1000
196	T	500-1000
197	T	300-500
	B	300-500
198	TR	300-500
	BR	300-500
199	B	500-1000
200	L	100-300
	TR	500-1000
	BR	300-500
201	TR	300-500
	BL	300-500
	BR	500-1000
202	BR	500-1000
203	TL	300-500
	TR	1000+
204	L	1000+
	TR	300-500
205	TL	300-500
	BL	300-500
	R	under $100
206	TL&R	100-300
	BL	300-500
207	T	300-500
	BL	100-300
	BR	500-1000
208	TL	200-300
	TR	300-500
	BL	300-500
	BR	400-500
209	T	1000+
210	L	300-500
	TR	300-500
	BR	300-500
211	TL	500-1000
	TR	300-500
	BL	300-500
	BR	500-1000
212	T	300-500
	BL	500-1000
	BR	300-500
213	L	500-1000
	TR	300-500
	BR	300-500
214	L	500-1000
	TR	300-500
	BR	300-500
215	TL	300-500

A mid-1920s ad for Lentheric perfumes.

249

Fragrance Names Index

General Index

1950's ad for *Arpege* by Lanvin, Paris.